Magic Tricks For Kids

79 Astonishing Magic Tricks For Kids

MAGIC SQUARES

To perform this trick you need a pencil and a paper.

First you have to draw 2 horizontal lines and 2 vertical lines, to make a tic tac toe board. You have to fill each square with numbers between 1 and 9 so that if you add the numbers in each column, row or diagonal the result should always be 15. If the numbers equal something else you should keep trying with different numbers.

Step by step
1. Draw a tic tac toe board (two horizontal line and 2 vertical line)
2. Fill each square in the board with a number between 1 and 9
3. Make sure that if you add the numbers in every column, row or diagonal the result is always 15
4. If the result is not 15 try again with replacing the numbers in the squares

1.)

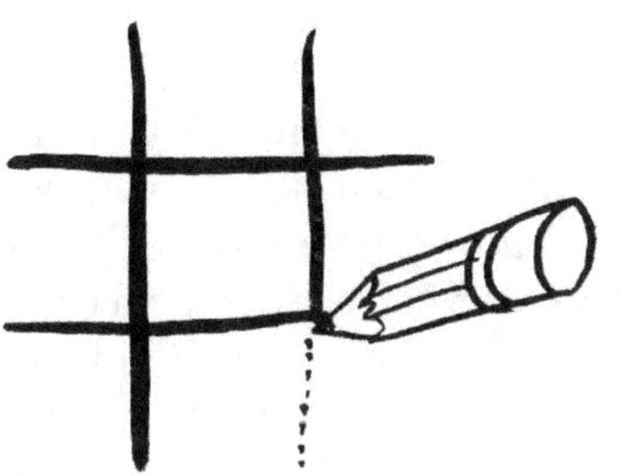

2.)

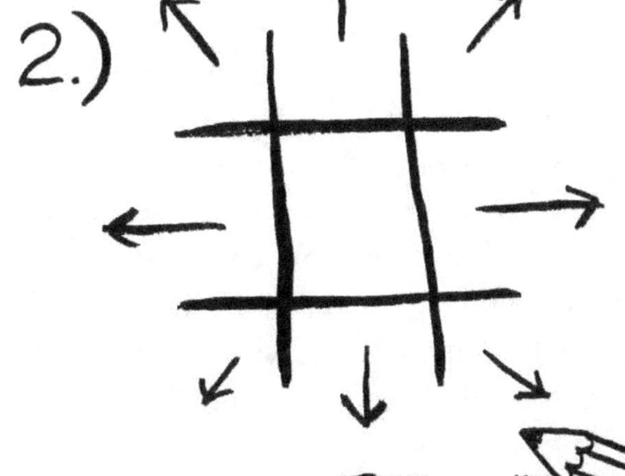

MIND READING

To perform this trick you need a piece of chewing gum and a magic partner.

Start the performance by telling everybody that you can read the mind of your partner. Ask someone in the audience to whisper a number between 1 and 10 in your partner's ear. Then put your hands on your partner's cheeks and act like you are reading his mind. Before the trick the partner should take a chewing gum and now he should chew his gum the same number of times as the number he was told in his ear. You just count the chews and say the number.

Step by step
1. Ask someone from the audience to help you and your partner
2. The member form the audience whispers your assistant a number between 1 and 10
3. Put your hands on your partner's cheek
4. Partner has to chew his chewing gum as many times as the helper's number is
5. Say the number

1.) 

2.) 

3.)

I KNOW YOUR NUMBER

To perform this trick you need some paper and 3 pens.

First you should fold the paper into thirds and tear it neatly along the folds, so you get three equal sized parts. Now you hand all three sheets into your audience (along with pens), but be careful to whom you give the middle sheet (it is ragged on both sides and is the most important sheet for this trick). Tell the participants to write a random number on the sheets and to really concentrate on these numbers. Then collect the sheets and scramble them. Now find the middle sheet (which is ragged on both sides), pull it up and ask the member of the audience to who you gave this sheet if this is his number.

Step by step
1. Fold the sheet of paper into thirds
2. Tear the paper along the folds (in three pieces)
3. Hand all three pieces to the audience
4. Tell the members of the audience that get the papers to write on them a random number
5. Collect back the sheets
6. Find out the middle sheet (it is ragged on both sides)

7. Pull the middle sheet up
8. Show it to the participant that it belongs to and tell him his secret number

ELEVEN FINGERS

To perform this trick you only need your hands. Start the performance by telling your audience that you have eleven fingers on your hands and you can prove it. First you count your fingers on your right hand with one, two, three, four and five. Then you count your fingers on your left hand with six, seven, eight, nine and ten. Now you act surprised and count them again only this time you count backwards. So you count your fingers on your left hand with ten, nine, eight, seven and six. Then stop, hold up your right hand and say: six plus five is eleven.

Step by step

1. Count the fingers on your right hand with one, two, three, four and five
2. Count the fingers on your left hand with six, seven, eight, nine and ten
3. Act surprised why there are only ten fingers
4. Start to count again – start on your left hand with ten, nine, eight, seven and six
5. Add the five fingers from your right hand to six and tell everybody that you have eleven fingers

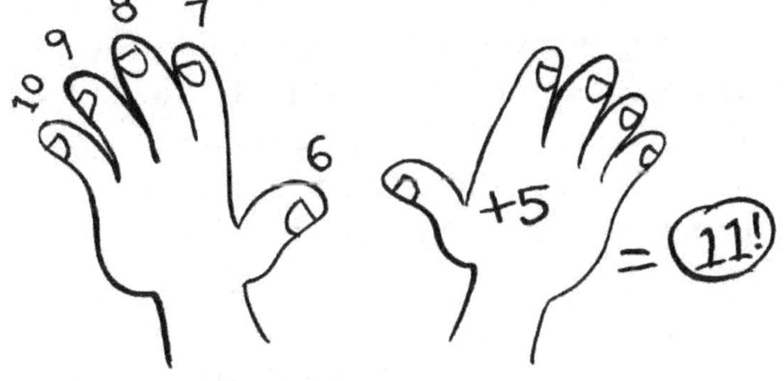
10
9
8
7
6
+5
= 11!

GUESS THE NUMBER

To perform this trick you need a pen and a paper. First you write a number on a paper – this calendar year times two (2017 x 2 = 4034). Now fold this paper and put it in your pocket. Now you give the pen and the paper to someone in the audience. Tell him to write down the year he was born in, then the year he graduated from high school (or the year he started at the school if he is still in the school), how old he will be at the end of this year and the number of years since the graduation (or the number of years he has been in school if he is still in the school). Now he should add up all this numbers and write down the result. Next you take out the paper on which you wrote your number and compare the results, which should be the same.

Step by step
1. Right down on a paper this calendar year times two (2017 x 2 = 4034)
2. Fold that paper and put it in the pocket
3. Ask someone in the audience to help you
4. Give him a paper and a pen

5. Tell him to write down the year he was born in, the year he graduated the high school in, how old he will be at the end of this year and the number of the years since the high school graduation
6. Tell him to add all this numbers
7. Compare your result to his result – they should be the same

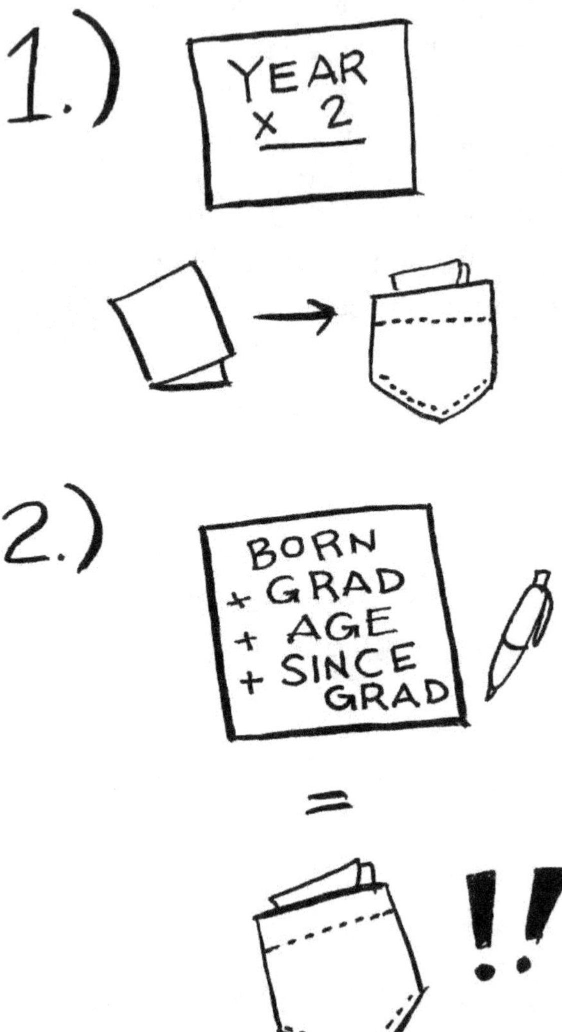

1.)
YEAR
x 2

2.)
BORN
+ GRAD
+ AGE
+ SINCE GRAD
=

GIMME 5

To perform this trick you need only an audience. Ask someone in the audience to pick a number. Then tell him to add the next number to it, next he should add 9 and divide by 2. For the end he shall have to subtract the original number. The result should always be 5.

Step by step
1. Ask someone in the audience to help you
2. Tell him to pick a number, but he can't tell you it
3. Tell him to add to his number the number next to it (result 1)
4. Tell him to add 9 to the result 1 (result 2)
5. Tell him to divide the result 2 with 2 (result 3)
6. Tell him to subtract the original number from the result 3
7. The final result should be 5

X + (X+1) = Y
Y + 9 = Z
Z ÷ 2 - X = 5

MIND READER

To perform this trick you need only an audience. Ask someone in the audience to pick a number between 2 and 9, but he can't tell you which number he picked. Now ask him to multiply this number by 9. Then he should add the two digits in the result and then subtract 5. Next tell him to think of a letter which is on that place in the alphabet (1-A, 2-B, …) and to think of a country that starts with that letter. Now tell him to think about animals that start with the next letter in the alphabet. Say to him that he is thinking about Elephants in Denmark as 95% of people will come up with those two things.

Step by step
1. Ask someone in the audience to help you
2. Tell him to pick a number between 2 and 9, but he can't tell you it
3. Tell him to multiply his number by 9 (result 1)
4. Tell him to add the two digits in the result 1 (result 2)
5. Tell him to subtract 5 from the result 2 (final result)
6. Tell him to think of a letter that is on that place (final result) in the alphabet

7. Tell him to think of a country that starts with that letter
8. Tell him to think about animal that starts with the next letter in the alphabet
9. Tell him he is thinking about Elephants in Denmark

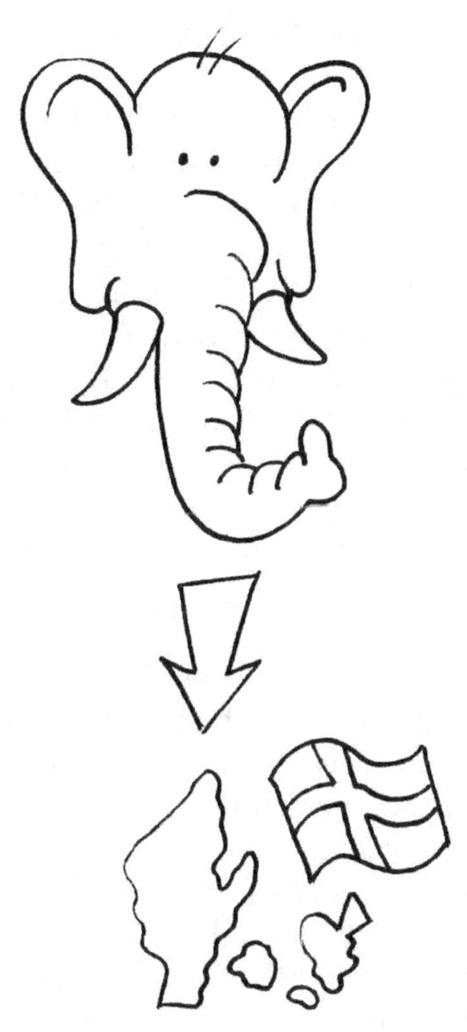

THE MAGIC NUMBER

To perform this trick you need a calculator.
First you should tell someone in the audience to think of a number between 1 and 100, but they can't tell you which number. Now you put in the calculator your age, multiply by 2, add 5, multiply by 50 and for the end subtract 365. Now you pass the calculator to the member of the audience and tell him to add to your number his secret number and then add 115, too. The first half of the result should be your age and the second half of the result should be his secret number.

Step by step
1. Ask someone in the audience to help you
2. Tell him to think of a number between 1 and 100, but he can't tell you the number
3. Take the calculator and put in your age
4. Multiply your age by 2 (result 1)
5. Add 5 to result 1 (result 2)
6. Multiply by 50 result 2 (result 3)
7. Subtract with 365 the result 3 (result 4)
8. Pass the calculator to the helper
9. Tell him to add his number to result 4 (result 5)
10. Tell him to add 115 to result 5 (final result)

11.Read the final result (first half of the result
   is you age, second half is your helper's
   secret number)

TURN WINE INTO WATER

To perform this trick you need two empty glasses, water, bleach and red food coloring.
First you should put a little bleach in one empty glass and fill the other glass with water and a few drops of red food coloring. Tell everybody that the red water is actually red wine and pour it to the glass with bleach. It should take back a neutral color.
IMPORTANT: Don't drink any of the liquids.

Step by step
1. Put a little bleach in empty glass
2. Fill the other glass with water
3. Pour a few drops of red coloring in the water
4. Pour the water with the coloring in the glass with bleach (the bleach will make water take back its original neutral color)

1.)
BLEACH
H₂O
2.)
RED
3.)

INVISIBLE STRING

To perform this trick you need a paper clip, a magnet and a thin cardboard.

First place a paper clip on a cardboard and tell the audience that you have a magical piece of string that is invisible. Next hold the magnet under the cardboard and let it attract the paper clip. Now you act like you have an invisible power to move the paper clip, but you only move the magnet under the cardboard and it actually moves the paper clip.

Step by step
1. Place a paper clip on a piece of cardboard
2. Hold the magnet under the cardboard and let it attract the paper clip
3. Move the magnet under the cardboard so the paper clip will move with it

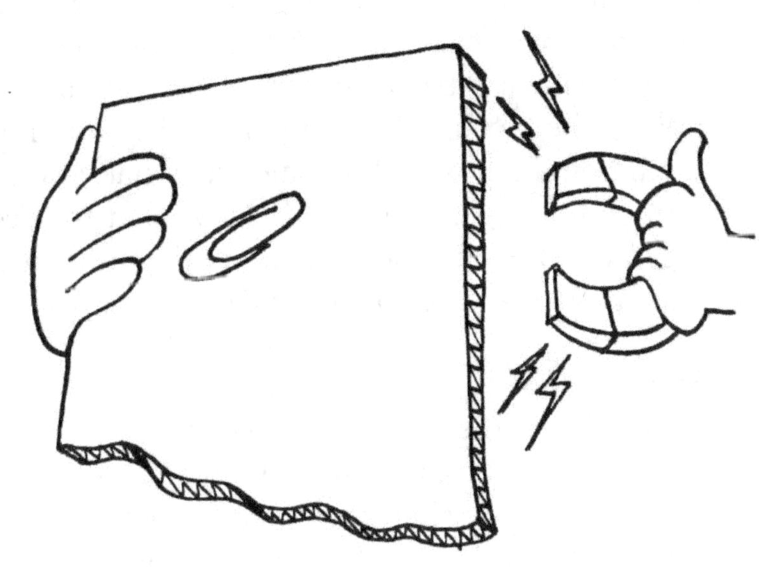

MUMMY FINGER

To perform this trick you need a piece of cotton, baby powder and a small gift box with lid.
Cut a hole in a bottom of the box, big enough to put your finger through. Then fill the box with the cotton so you can't see the hole. Now dust your finger with the baby powder, put it through the hole in the box and lay it down on the cotton. Put the lid on the box, tell the audience that you have a mummy finger in it and if they want to see it. Open the box and show them the finger. You can also move it a little so the effect will be stronger.

Step by step
1. Cut a hole in the bottom of the box
2. Fill the box with the cotton
3. Dust your finger with a baby powder
4. Put your finger through the hole and lay it down on the cotton
5. Put the lid on the box
6. Open the box and show the audience your finger (a mummy finger)
7. Move the finger for a bigger effect

1.)

2.)

3.)

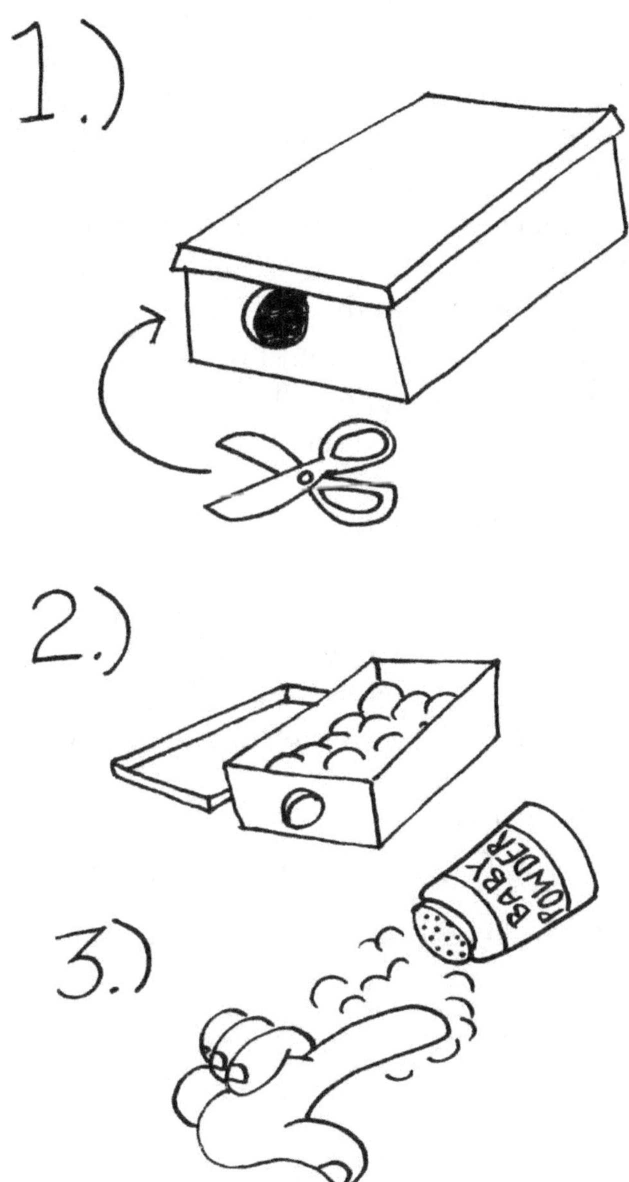

INVISIBLE INK

To perform this trick you need paper, table lamp paintbrush and a lemon, orange or apple juice.
First dip your paintbrush into a juice and write a message on a piece of paper. Wait a few minutes so that the juice dries and the message will disappear. Give the paper to someone in the audience and have him hold it close to the table lamp (normal lightbulb) and your message should magically appear again.

Step by step
1. Dip the paintbrush into a juice
2. Write a message on the paper with it
3. Wait for a few minutes so the juice dries and the message disappears
4. Give the paper to a member in the audience
5. Tell him to hold the paper close to the table lamp (the message will reappear)

1.) 

2.) 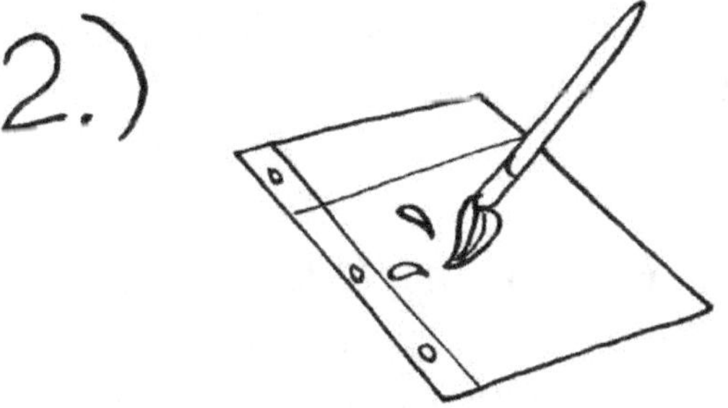

3.) 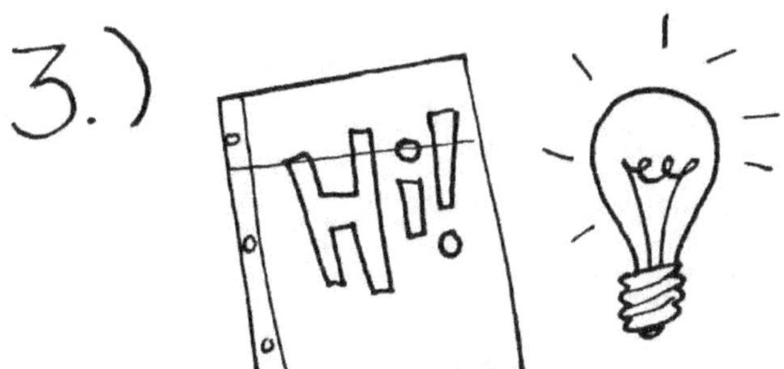

MONEY ROLL OVER

To perform this trick you need two money bills of different value.

First you place a bill on the table in front of you. Now place the other bill perpendicularly on the first bill and make sure that the edges are lined up. Next you roll up both bills, you start at the bottom. After that you act like you are doing magic. Now you unroll the and because of the way of unrolling the bills flip in the process. You make the bills switched their positions.

Step by step
1. Place one bill on the table in front of you
2. Place the other bill perpendicularly on the first bill, edges lined up
3. Roll up both bills
4. Unroll the bills

1.)

2.)

3.)

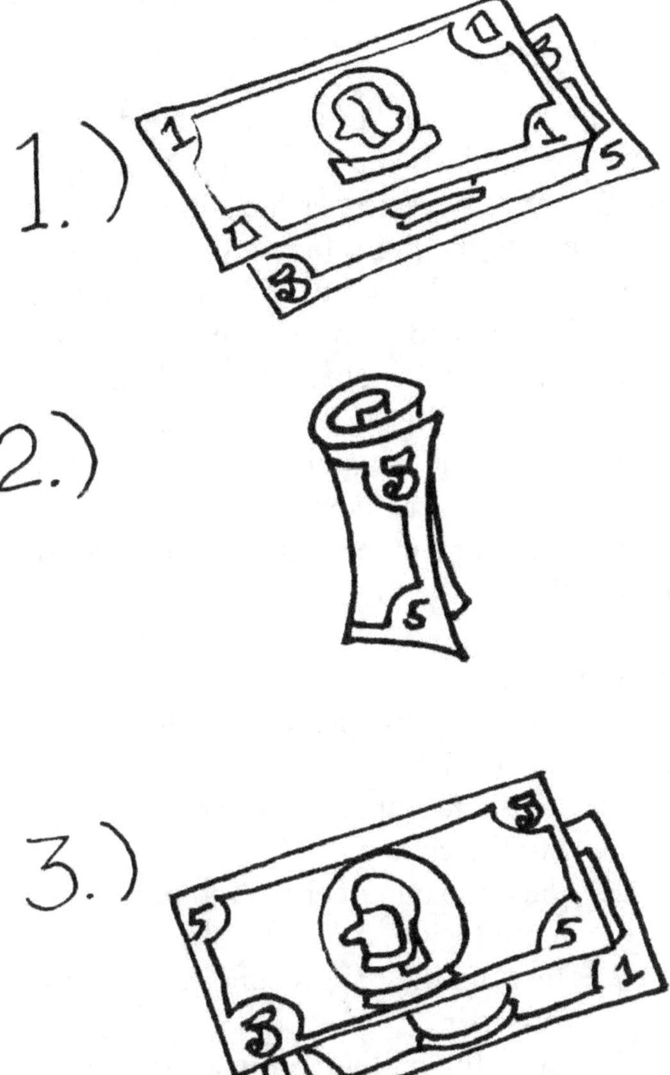

MOVE A TOOTHPICK WITHOUT TOUCHING IT

To perform this trick you need a balloon, thumbtack, plastic cup and a flat toothpick.
At first you have to set the thumbtack on a flat surface with the point facing up. Next you put the toothpick on the point of the thumbtack and carefully balance it to the center. Now place the cup (it should be clear, not colored) over the toothpick and the thumbtack. Next blow up the balloon and rub it against your hair to make a static electricity. Move the balloon around the cup and it will make the toothpick move without even touching it.

Step by step
1. Place a thumbtack (point facing up) on a flat surface
2. Put the toothpick on the point and balance it to the center
3. Place the cup over the toothpick (and thumbtack)
4. Blow up the balloon and rub it against your hair
5. Move the balloon around the cup so it will make move the toothpick, too

1.)

2.)

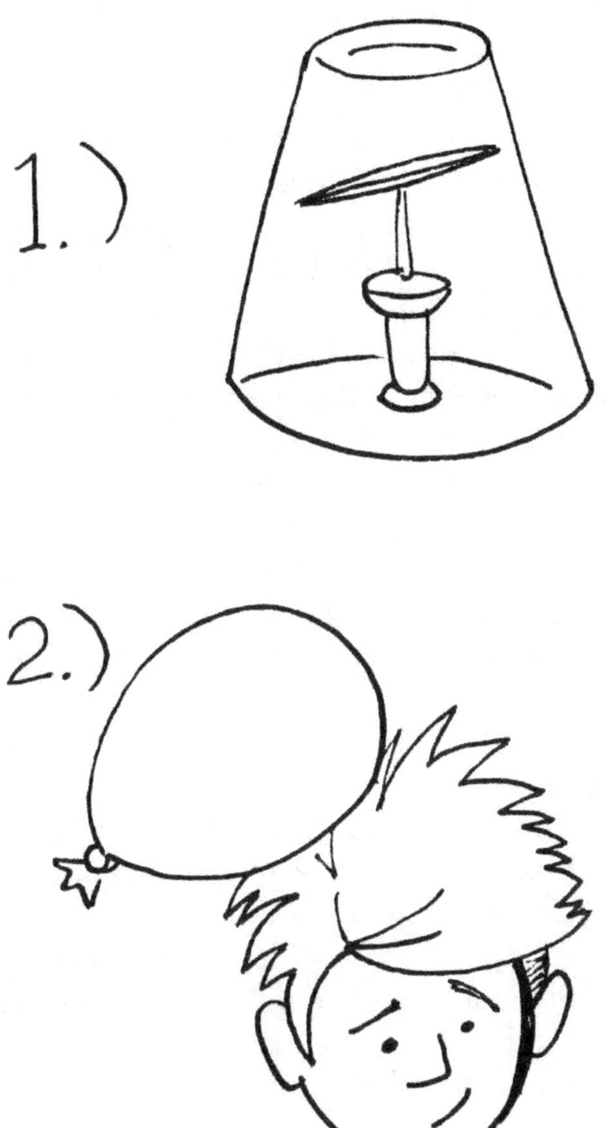

DISAPPEARING COIN

To perform this trick you need a large coin.
For start you put your left hand on the back of your neck and tell the audience that you can make the coin disappear with just rubbing it on your elbow. Start doing it – rubbing the coin on your left elbow for a few seconds. After that remove your hand and let the coin drop on the floor. Act surprised and tell the audience that the trick didn't work and you will try again. Pick up the coin with your left hand and pretend that you put it in your right hand. Make the trick again only now you drop the coin down to your t-shirt (with your left hand). For the end stop rubbing your elbow and remove your hand to show to everybody that you make the coin disappear.

Step by step
1. Rub the coin on your left elbow
2. Remove your hand and let the coin fall on the floor
3. Pick up the coin with you left hand
4. Pretend that you out the coin in your right hand
5. Make the rubbing again
6. Drop the coin down to your t-shirt
7. Stop the rubbing and remove your hand

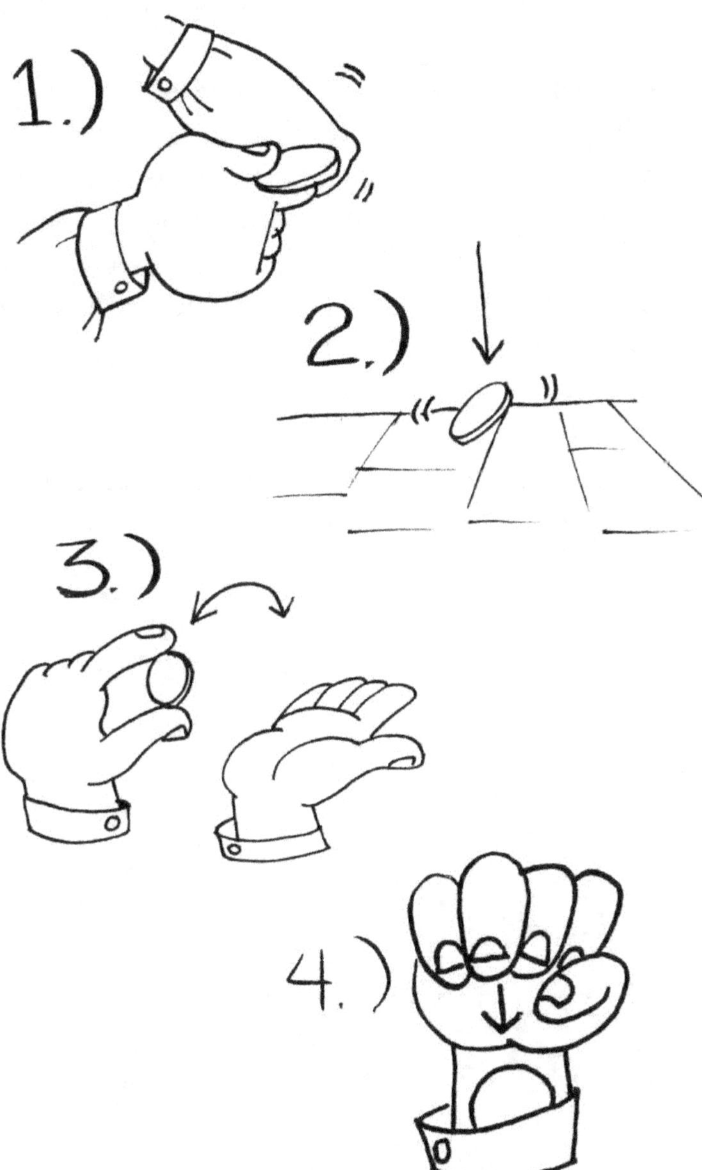
1.)
2.)
3.)
4.)

THE AMAZING FLOATING EGG TRICK

To perform this trick you need an egg, ½ cup of salt and a glass filled with water.
At first you put the egg in the water and show everybody how it sinks to the bottom. Now pour the salt in water and mix it so the salt dissolves. It will make the egg float, because the density of the water thickens.

Step by step
1. Put the egg in the water and let it sink
2. Pour the salt in water
3. Mix the water

1.)

2.)

3.)

LIFT AN ICE CUBE WITH A PIECE OF STRING

To perform this trick you need a salt shaker, piece of string ice cube and a glass of water.

Ask someone in the audience to help you with the performance. Hand to him all the things you prepared – glass of water with an ice cube in it, piece of string and a salt shaker. Tell him to lift the ice cube from the water without even touching the glass. When he gives up (he will for sure) you show him and everybody else how this thing is done. Lay the string across the ice cube, sprinkle a little salt on the ice and wait. After a minute pull the string and the ice cube should come out with it as well.

Step by step
1. Ask someone in the audience to help you
2. Tell him to lift the ice cube from the water without touching the glass
3. Lay the string across the ice cube
4. Sprinkle a little salt on the ice cube
5. Wait a minute
6. Pull the string

1.)

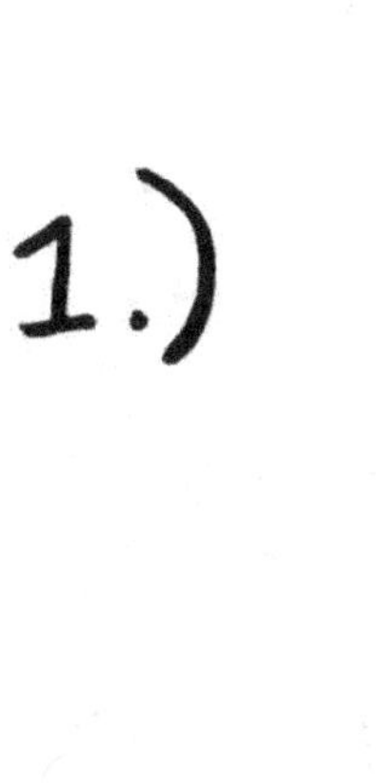

2.)

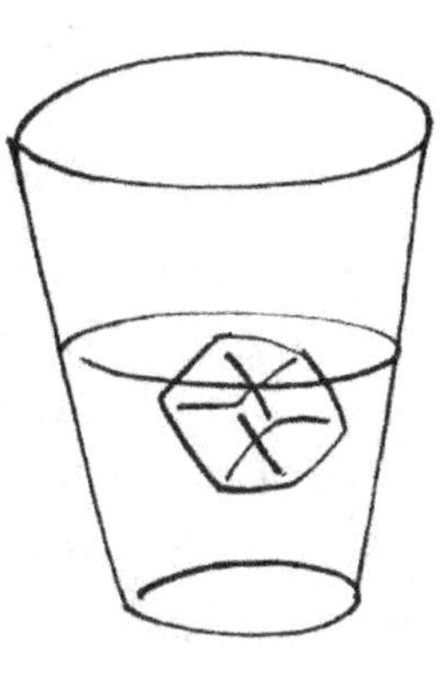

3.)

 1:00

MAGNETIC COMB

To perform this trick you need a ping pong ball, plastic comb and a paper.

First you tell your audience that you have a magic magnetic comb. Now you rip up the paper into small pieces. Next you rub the comb against your hair, to charge it with static electricity, and move it over the pieces of paper, so they jump onto the comb. After that you recharge the comb, with by rubbing it again through your hair. Now you place a ping pong ball on a desk and bring the comb close to it. The ball should start to move towards the comb.

Step by step
1. Rip up the paper into small pieces
2. Rub the comb to your hair
3. Move the comb over the pieces of paper
4. Rub the comb to your hair, again
5. Place a ping pong ball on the table
6. Bring the comb close to the ping pong ball

1.)

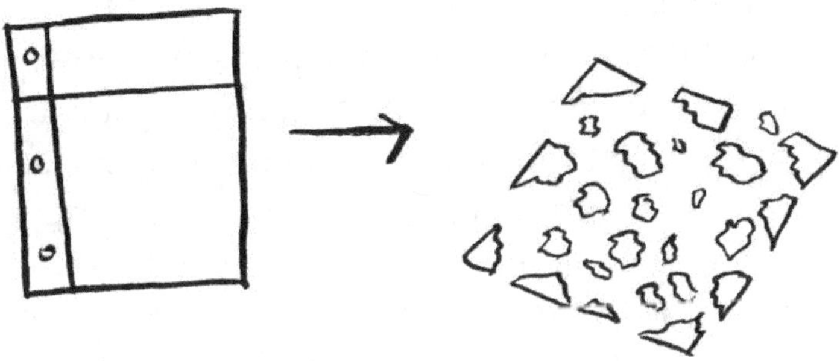

2.)

LEVITATING BUTTER KNIFE

To perform this trick you need a wristwatch and a butter knife (the one with no sharp edges).

First you tell the audience that you can move a butter knife above the table with using just your mental powers. Now put the knife down at the table and your hand (on which you have a watch) over it, palm down. Say some magic words (act like you are making magic) and wiggle your fingers. As you do that push the butter knife under the strap of your wristwatch. Now raise your hand and slowly move it so the knife will raise and move, too.

Step by step
1. Put the knife on the table
2. Put your hand over the knife
3. Wiggle your fingers
4. As you wiggle your fingers push the butter knife under the strap of your wristwatch
5. Raise your hands a little
6. Move your hand and the knife with it

1.)

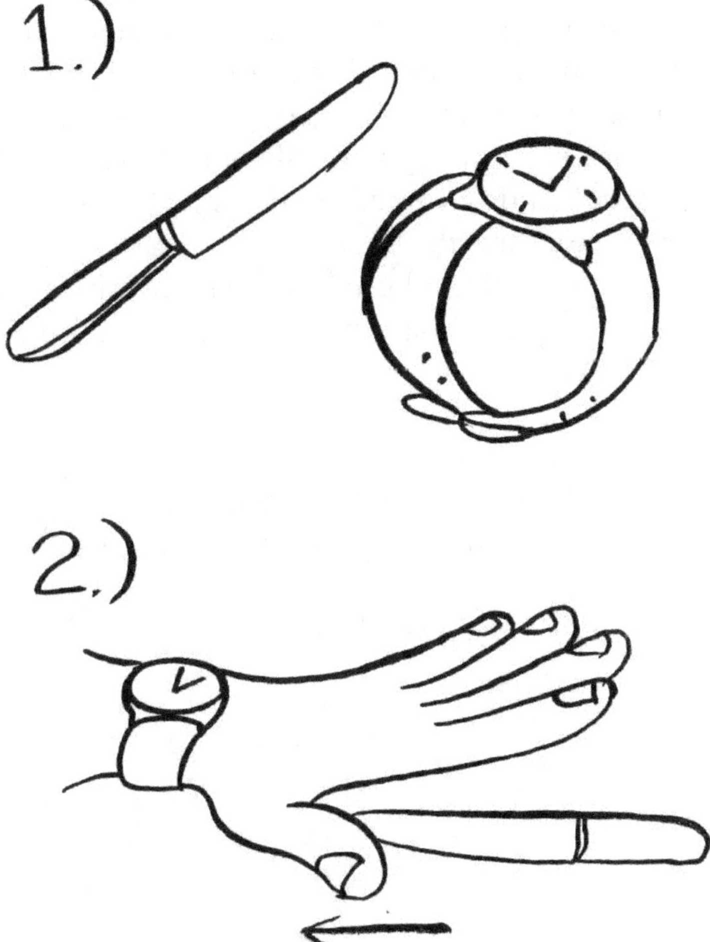

2.)

CAN YOU CRACK AN EGG?

To perform this trick you need an egg.
Take an egg into your hand and tighten your grip to the point of smashing it. Because of the design of the egg the pressure will spread all over the area so you can now try with all your strength to smash the egg and if you are doing it right you will not be able to smash it.
Make sure that you don't have any rings or any other objects that can make the egg smash by themselves.

Step by step
1. Take an egg in your hand
2. Tighten your grip to the point of smashing it
3. Try to smash the egg

CAN YOU PICK UP THIS DOLLAR BILL?

To perform this trick you need a dollar bill and a wall.

Ask someone in the audience to help you with this trick. Put him in front of the wall with his heels touching it. Now place the dollar bill on the floor in front of him. Then tell him to try to pick up the dollar bill without moving his feet or bending the knees. He won't be able to do it.

Step by step
1. Ask someone in the audience to help you
2. Place him in front of the wall
3. Place the dollar bill on the floor in front of the helper
4. Tell him to pick up the dollar bill without moving his feet or bending his knees

THE COIN VANISH

To perform this trick you need a dark scarf, rubber band and a quarter coin.

First you have to put a small rubber band around your thumb and next three fingers on your left hand. Hold your left hand in pocket so nobody can see the rubber band. Next you pull out the scarf with your right hand and smoothly drape it over your left hand. Place the coin on the scarf. Now fold the scarf and while doing that open your fingers to capture the coin with just a small amount of the scarf. Next you remove your fingers from the rubber band as it is capturing the coin. Let the scarf fall on the floor.

Step by step

1. Put a small rubber band around your thumb and next three fingers on your left hand
2. Put your left hand in your pocket
3. Pull out the scarf and cover your left hand with it
4. Place the coin on the scarf
5. Fold the scarf
6. Open your fingers and capture the coin and a small amount of the scarf
7. Remove your fingers from the rubber band
8. Let the scarf fall on the floor

1.)

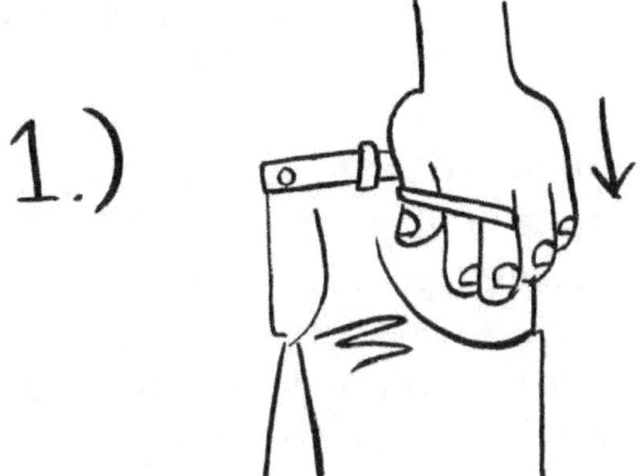

2.)

3.)

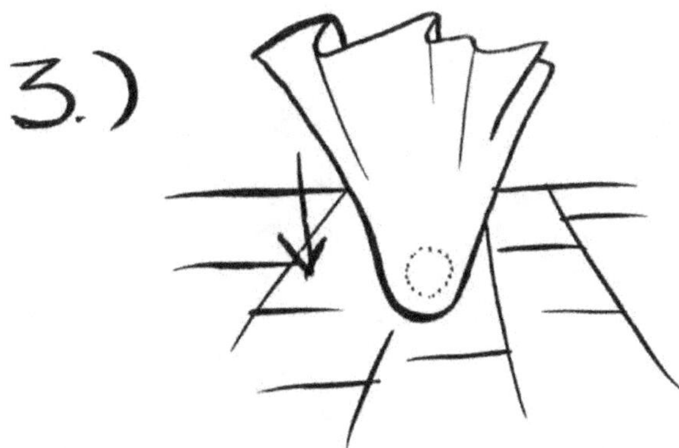

CAN YOU PUT TWO PEN POINTS TOGETHER?

To perform this trick you need 2 pens.
Ask someone in the audience to hold one pen in each hand, so the pens are pointing to each other. Now tell him to close one eye and try to put the pens together. It will be very hard for him to do that so he will have to try more times. You can make a bet in how many times he can do it.

Step by step
1. Ask someone in the audience to help you
2. Tell him to hold one pen in each hand
3. Tell him to close one eye
4. Tell him to put the pens together

CAN YOU BLOW UP THIS BALLOON?

To perform this trick you need an empty soda bottle and a balloon.
Place a balloon inside of a soda bottle and wrap its opening around the hole of the bottle. Now bet with someone in the audience that he can't blow up this balloon for no matter what. He really won't be able to do it because the bottle is full of air and there is no space left over for the balloon to expand.

Step by step
1. Ask someone in the audience to help you
2. Place a balloon inside of a soda bottle
3. Wrap the balloon's opening around the hole of the bottle
4. Tell the helper to blow up the balloon

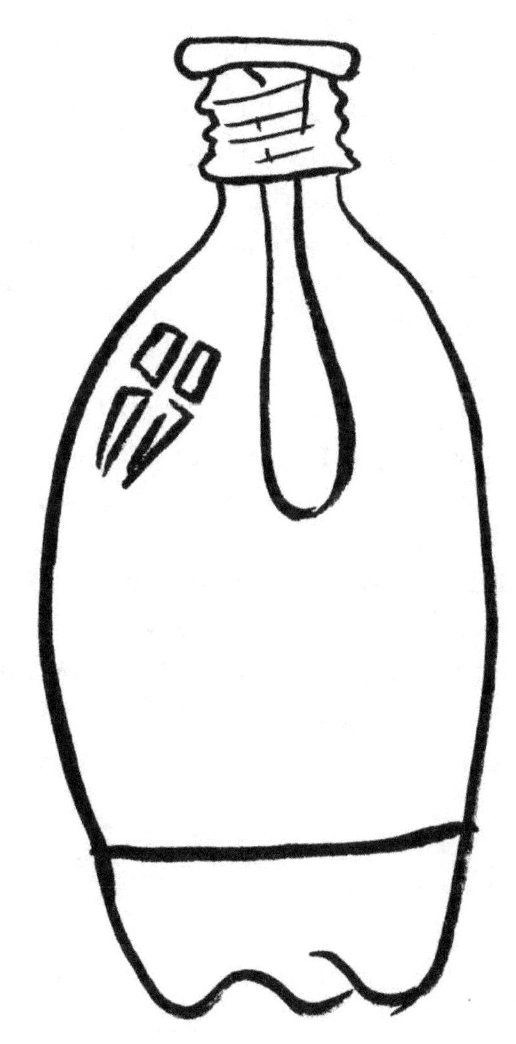

CAN YOU PUSH ME AROUND?

To perform this trick you need a broom.
Ask someone in the audience to help you. Give him a broom to hold it with both hands (fully stretched). Now you put one hand on the broom and tell him to try to push you away. As he pushes forward you push upwards and so you neutralize all his force. He won't be able to move you, not even a centimeter.

Step by step
1. Ask someone in the audience to help you
2. Tell him to hold the broom with both his hands
3. Put one hand to the broom
4. Tell him to push you away
5. When he pushes you away you push the broom upwards

1.)

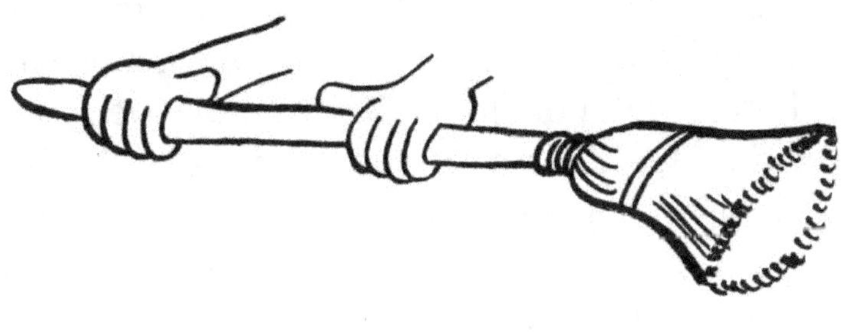

2.)

THE COIN PYRAMID

To perform this trick you need ten identical coins. First you have to make a pyramid with your ten coins. Ask someone in the audience to invert the pyramid with only three moves, so they can move only one coin at the time. After they give up show them how this is done. First move is to switch the bottom-left coin to the 2nd from the top row on the right side. Second move is to move the bottom-right coin again to the 2nd from the top row on the right side. And the final move is to move the top coin to the center of the bottom.

Step by step
1. Ask someone in the audience to help you
2. Make a coin pyramid with 10 coins
3. Tell the helper to invert your pyramid
4. Give him a few minutes to try
5. Switch the bottom-left coin to the 2nd from the top row on thr right side
6. Move the bottom-right coin to the 2nd from the top row on the right side
7. Move the top coin to the center of the bottom

1.)  × **10**

2.)

3.)

CAN YOU TIE A KNOT?

To perform this trick you need a two foot long piece of rope.

Bet someone in the audience that he can't make a knot with a rope without letting go of either of the ends of the rope. Leave him to try for a while. Then you take the rope, but first you cross your arms in front of your chest. Grab each end of the rope in one hand and slowly unfold your arms. You will automatically make a knot.

Step by step
1. Ask someone in the audience to help you
2. Tell him to tie a tie a knot with a rope without letting go either of the rope's ends
3. Cross your arms in front of your chest
4. Grab each end of the rope with one hand
5. Unfold your arms

1.)

2 ft.

2.)

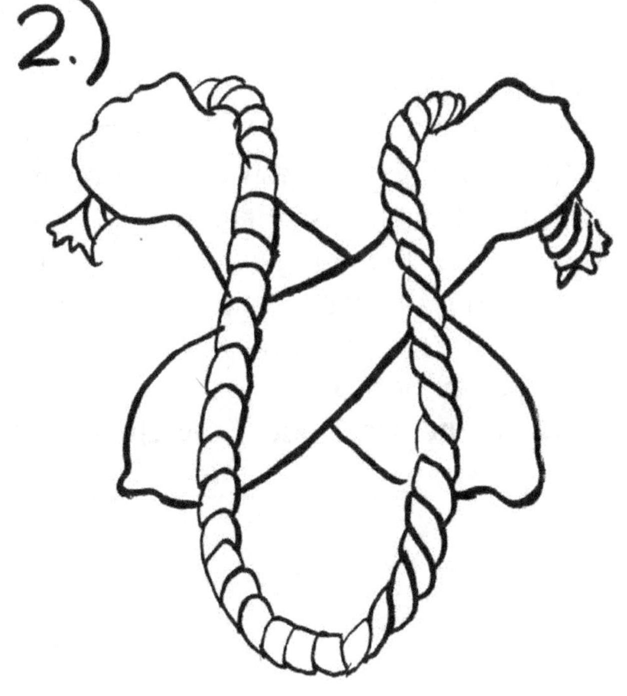

WATER BET

To perform this trick you need a hat and a glass of a water.

First you put the glass on the table and hat over it. Now tell the audience that you can drink the water out of the glass without touching the hat. Go under the table and make a sound like you are really drinking the water. Now ask somebody from the audience to check if the glass is really empty. When he pulls up the hat you simply take the glass and drink all the water.

Step by step
1. Ask someone in the audience to help you
2. Put the glass with a water on the table
3. Cover the glass with a hat
4. Go under the table and act like you are drinking the water out of the glass
5. Tell the helper to check if there is still a water in the glass
6. Drink the water out of the glass

1.)

2.)

3.)

CAN YOU GET THE DIME?

To perform this trick you need a dime, cork and an empty bottle.
First put the dime in the bottle and the cork in the bottle's hole. Now bet someone in the audience that he can't take the dime out of the bottle without pulling out the cork, too. After a few minutes of him trying, take the bottle, push the cork inside of it and shake the dime out.

Step by step
1. Ask someone in the audience to help you
2. Put the dime in the bottle
3. Put the cork in the bottle's hole
4. Tell your helper he has to get a dime out of the bottle without pulling the cork
5. Take the bottle
6. Push the cork inside
7. Shake out the dime

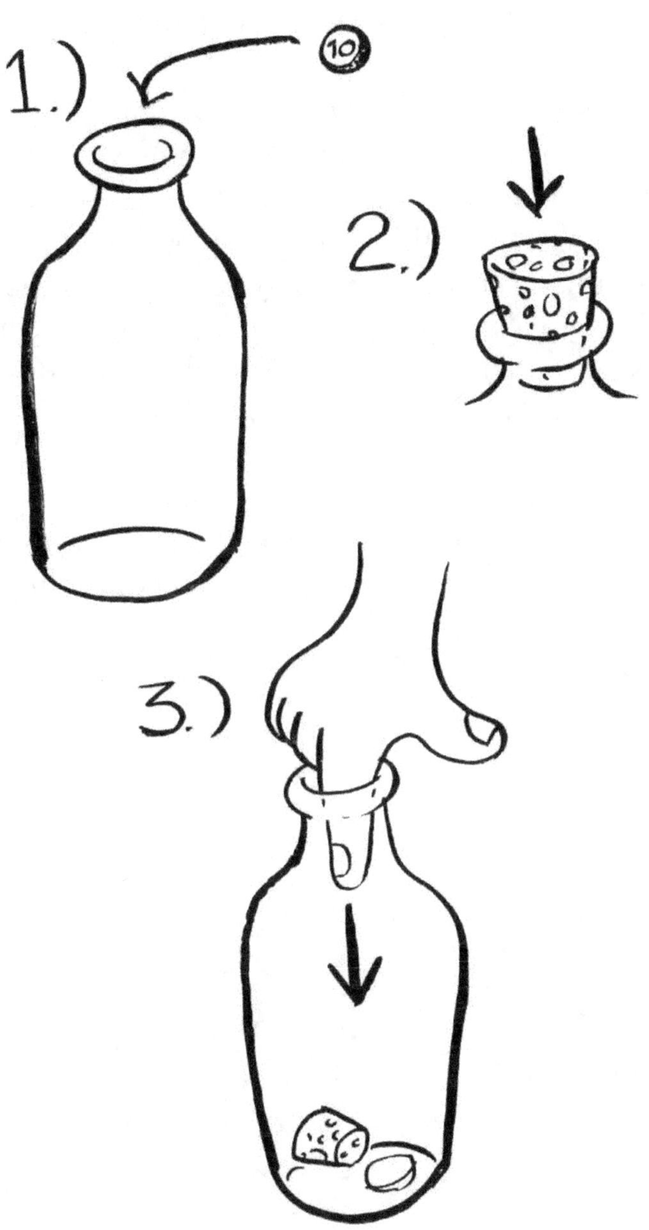

1.)
10
2.)
3.)

PLATE THROUGH FINGERS

To perform this trick you need a plate.
Ask someone in the audience to help you. Bet with him that you can push a plate through two of their fingers. He will think that is impossible, of course. But this is just a word play. So you just have to stick your finger between his two fingers (it doesn't' matter which two) and simply push the plate around.

Step by step
1. Ask someone in the audience to help you
2. Stick your finger between his two fingers
3. Push the plate

MAGIC COLORS PEN

To perform this trick you need a paper and a pen. Bet with someone in the audience that your pen can write down any color that he says. When he says a color you simply write down the color name and the trick is done, you wrote the color he said.

Step by step
1. Ask someone in the audience to help you
2. Ask him what color you should write down
3. Write down the color he says

PHANTOM COIN

To perform this trick you need two large coins. First you put two coins between your index fingers and hold them like that. Now you rub the coins together up and down very quickly. The effect should be like there is a third coin between your two coins.

Step by step
1. Put two coins between your index fingers
2. Rub the coins together up and down

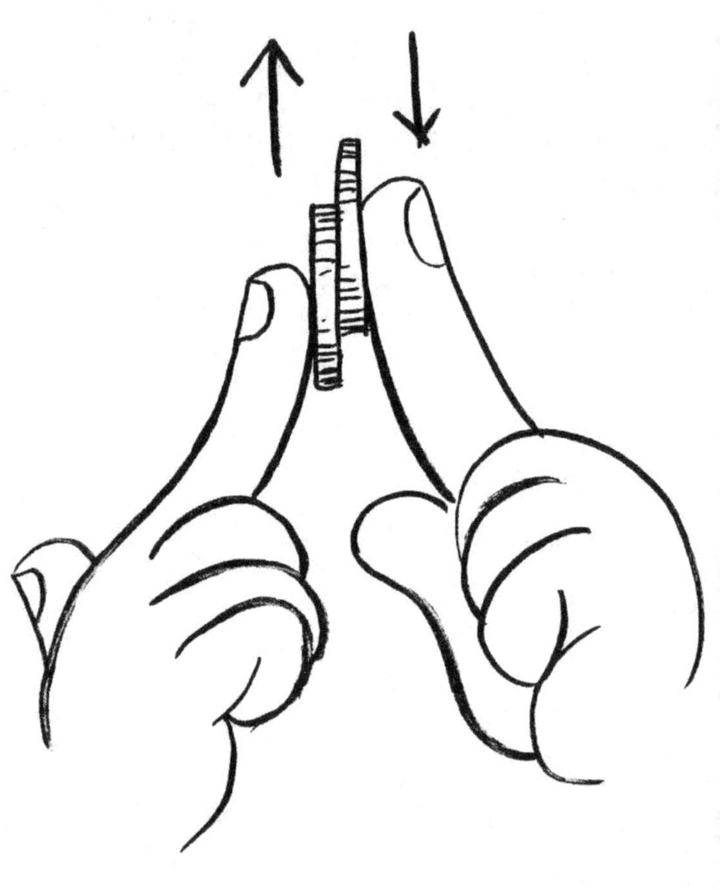

RUBBER PEN

To perform this trick you need a pen.
Hold the pen near its tip between your thumb and forefinger. Move your hand up and down so the pen moves with it. The whole thing should make your pen look like it has turned into rubber. The faster you will move your hand up and down the biggest the effect will be.

Step by step
1. Hold the pen between your thumb and forefinger
2. Move your hand up and down

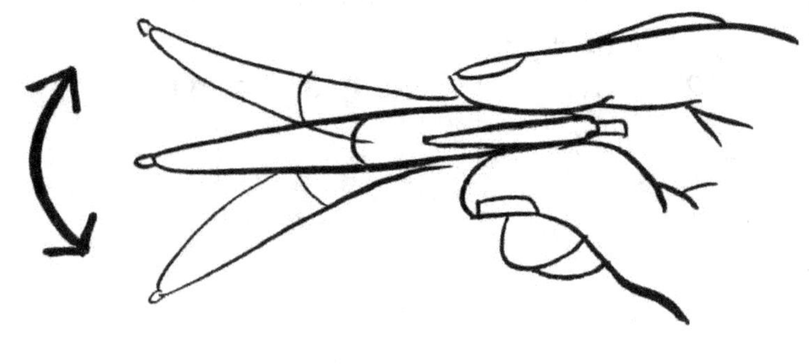

HOLE IN THE HANDS

To perform this trick you need a cardboard paper towel tube.

Bet with someone in the audience that you will make him see through his hand. Tell him to close his eyes, take the cardboard paper towel tube and place it on his right eye. Now he has to put his hand at the other end of the tube, with the palm facing his face. Now tell him to open his eyes and he will see that a hole has been "created" in his hand.

Step by step
1. Ask someone in the audience to help you
2. Tell him to close his eyes
3. Place the cardboard paper towel tube on his right eye
4. Tell him to put his hand at the other end of the tube
5. Tell him to open his eyes

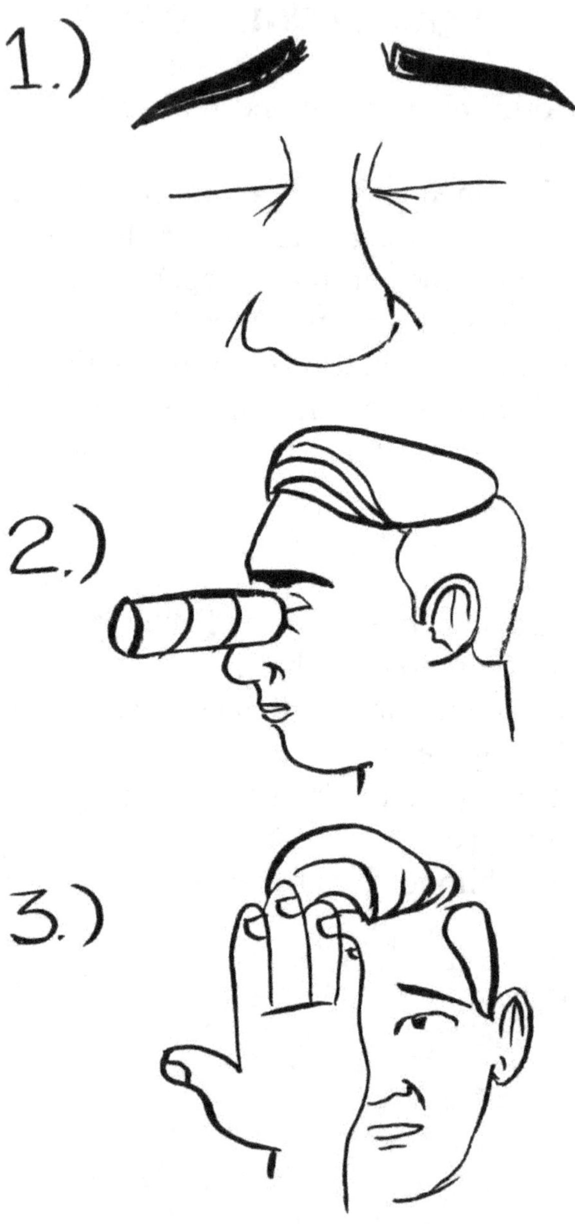

1.)
2.)
3.)

TEAR A COIN IN HALF

To perform this trick you need a large coin, an envelope and a tin foil.

First you have to cut the corners of the envelope so you get a square pouch. Next you cover the coin with the foil and press really hard on it so the coin leaves its mark onto the foil. Now open the foil, take the coin out and carefully fold the foil back. Now show the fake coin to the audience, put it in the pouch and rip everything up. Everybody will think that you ripped up the coin.

Step by step
1. Cut the corner of the envelope
2. Cover the coin with the foil
3. Press on the foil to make the coin leave a mark on it
4. Open the foil and take the coin out
5. Carefully fold the foil back
6. Put the fake coin in the pouch
7. Tear the pouch

1.)

2.)

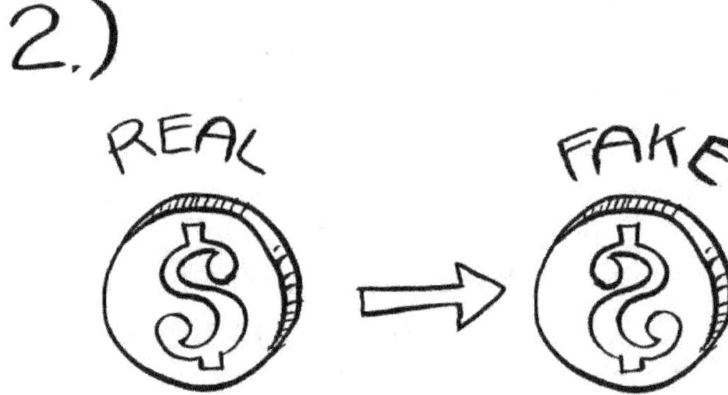

3.)

INVISIBLE STRING

To perform this trick you need two pencils (with the erasers at the end).

Ask someone in the audience to help you with the trick. Give him two pencils, each in one hand, with the erasers facing each other, and ask him to push them together as hard as he can. While he is pushing the pencils together you act like you are rolling some piece of string around the pencils. Do this act for at least 30 seconds. After half a minute his muscles will get used to that position so he will have a difficult time to move the pencils apart. When you tell him to do that it will seem like the pencils are tied together.

Step by step
1. Ask someone in the audience to help you
2. Give him a pencil in each hand
3. Tell him to point the erasers on the pencils against each other
4. Tell him to push the pencils together
5. Act like you are rolling a string around the pencils
6. Wait thirty seconds
7. Tell him to move the pencils apart

1.)

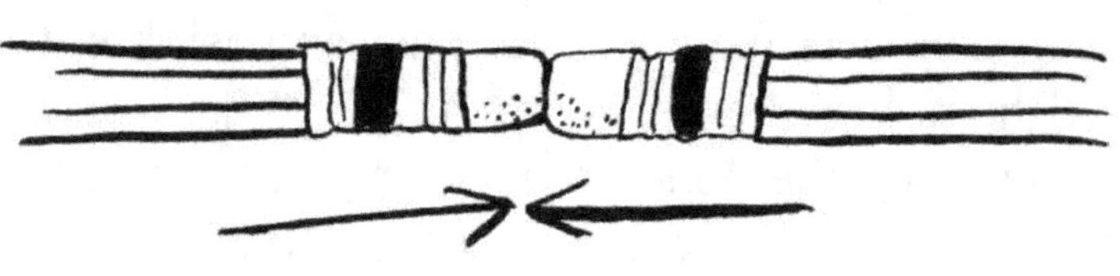

2.)

:30

POPPING STRAW

To perform this trick you need a straw.
First you pinch both ends of the straw, very strongly. Now twist the straw as many times as you can. At the middle it should be one untwisted part of the straw. Now ask someone in the audience to flick his finger at the untwisted part of the straw. Because of all the air that was captured in that part of the straw the flick will make a loud popping noise.

Step by step
1. Ask someone in the audience to help you
2. Pinch a straw on both ends of it
3. Twist the straw
4. Tell the helper to flick the untwisted part of the straw

1.)

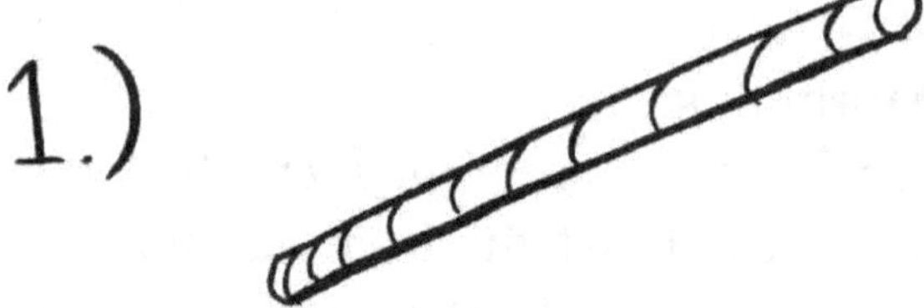

2.)

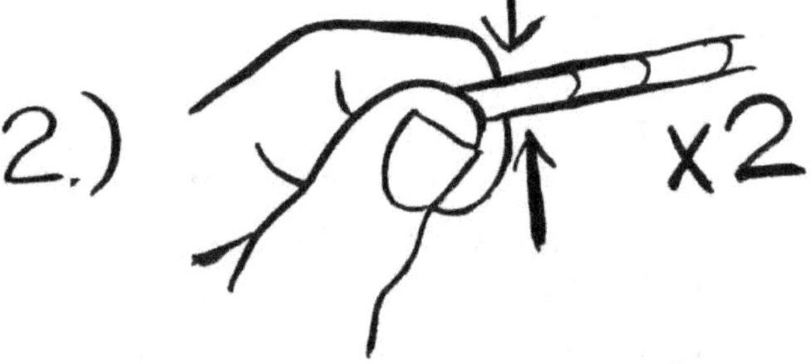

3.)

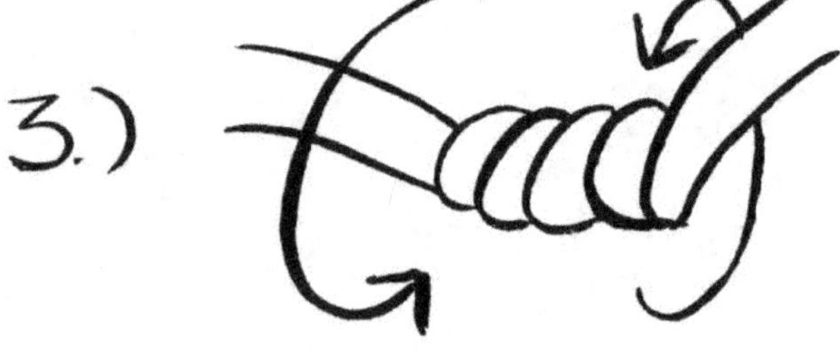

THE MAGICAL MOVING PEN

To perform this trick you need a pen (it must be round) and a table.

At first you take a pen, rub it on your sleeve and put in on the table in front of you. Place your hand over the pen with your finger pointing out (no touch) and act like you are going to move the pen only with your mental power. Secretly blow on the pen so it will start moving. Everybody will be amazed as they think you are moving the pen with your mental energy.

Step by step
1. Take a pen
2. Rub the pen on your sleeve
3. Put the pen on the table in front of you
4. Place your hand over the pen with your finger pointing out towards it
5. Secretly blow on the pen

1.)

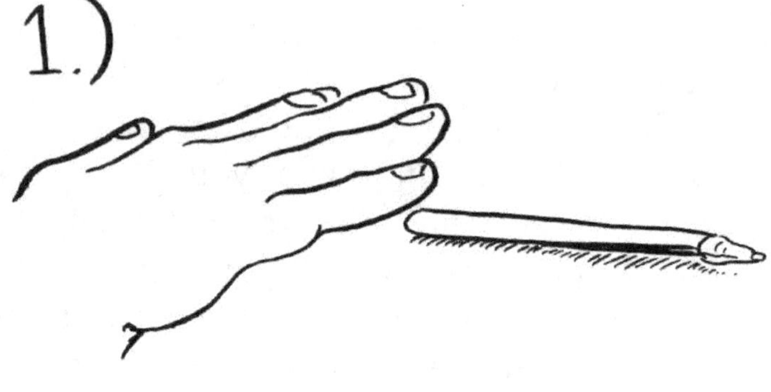

2.)

DISAPPEARING COIN

To perform this trick you need a coin, handkerchief, pen, 2 sheets of paper, plastic cup (clear, not colored) and a scissors.

First you have to place a cup on a sheet of paper (facing upside down) and trace around it with the pen. Now cut out the circle and glue it to the mouth of the cup. Put the coin and a cup (upside down) next to it on the other sheet of paper. Cover the coin and the cup with the handkerchief. Bet with the audience that you can make a coin disappear when you put a cup over it. Move the cup on the top of the coin and remove the handkerchief. Because the coin is hidden under the paper you glued to the mouth of the cup the coin will disappear.

Step by step
1. Place a cup on a sheet of paper
2. Trace around the cup with a pen
3. Cut out the circle
4. Glue the circle to the mouth of a cup
5. Put a coin and a cup on the other sheet of paper
6. Cover the coin and a cup with a handkerchief
7. Move the cup on the top of the coin
8. Remove the handkerchief

1.)

2.)

3.)

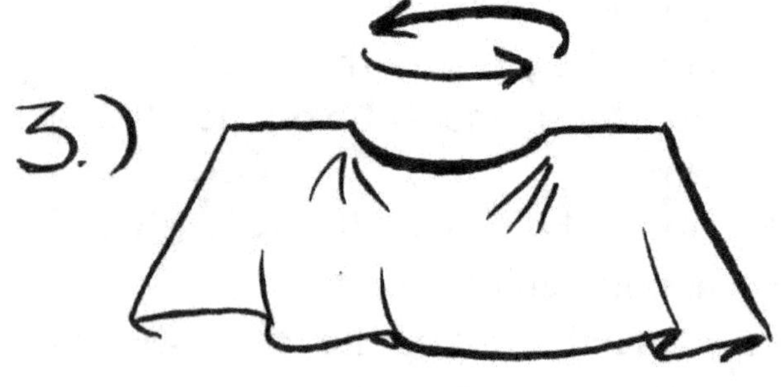

A REAL DRINKING CUP

To perform this trick you need a sponge, pitcher of water and a colored cup.
First you have to put a sponge in the bottom of the cup. Make sure it can't fall out if you move the cup. Pour a little water into the cup, wait for a few seconds so the sponge absorbs the water and make everyone believe that you have a magical cup.

Step by step
1. Put a sponge in the cup
2. Pour a water in the cup
3. Wait a few seconds
4. Turn the cup upside down

1.)

2.)

3.)

WALK THROUGH A SHEET OF PAPER

To perform this trick you need a piece of paper and a scissors.

Bet with your audience that you can cut a hole in a normal piece of paper big enough to walk through. You can ask someone to try by himself to do that. After they give up take the paper and the scissors and start cutting the paper. First you fold the paper and you start cutting it horizontally, not all the way through (start on the folded side). Turn the paper around and do the same thing on the other (unfolded) side. Now cut through the folded parts of the papers except the first and the last ones. That will keep your paper together as you will make a big circle out of it. Now unfold the paper, reveal your big hole and walk through it.

Step by step
1. Ask someone in the audience to help you
2. Tell him to cut the hole in the paper to walk through it
3. Wait a few minutes
4. Take the paper and fold it
5. Start cutting the paper, horizontally on the folded side, but not all the way through
6. Cut other side (unfolded) side the same way

7. Cut through the folded parts, except the first and last ones
8. Unfold the paper
9. Walk through the hole

DISAPPEARING MATCHSTICKS

To perform this trick you need two boxes of matches and a rubber band.

First you have to attach a box of matches to your wrist (using a rubber band) and hide it under your sleeve. Now show to the audience the other box of matches (the box should be empty) and shake it a little bit. Ask the audience how many matches do they think are in the box. Because of the sound of the matches that are in the box which is attached to your wrist they will think that the box in your hand is full with matches and they will all be wrong.

Step by step
  1. Attach a box of matches to your wrist
  2. Hide the box in your sleeve
  3. Pick up the other box of matches
  4. Shake your hand
  5. Ask the audience how many matches are in the box in your hand
  6. Open the box and show it to the audience

1.)

2.)

3.)

THE AMAZING ENVELOPE

To perform this trick you need a paper, markers, two identical envelopes and clear tape.

Tape two envelopes together along their sides with the clear tape, so it looks as if there is only one envelope. Draw a picture and make a copy of it, so you have two identical pictures. Put one of the pictures in the front envelope. Now bet with the audience that you can repair a torn-up picture. Now tear up the other picture and put the pieces in the other envelope (show that it is empty before you do it). Act you are doing magic and pull the other picture from the other envelope that it isn't torn-up.

Step by step
1. Tape two envelopes together
2. Draw a picture and make a copy of it
3. Put one of the pictures in the front envelope
4. Tear up the other picture and put the pieces in the other envelope
5. Take out the whole picture from the front envelope

1.)

2.) × 2

3.)

QUARTER IN THE EAR

To perform this trick you need a quarter.
First you have to take a quarter in your hand and put it behind your back. Tell someone in the audience that you see something shiny behind his ear. Now reach out with your hand behind his ear and act like you are pulling a quarter from it.

Step by step
1. Ask someone in the audience to help you
2. Hold a quarter
3. Put the quarter behind your back
4. Tell your helper he has something shiny behind his ear
5. Reach out with your hand behind your helper's ear
6. Act like you pull a quarter from his ear

1.)

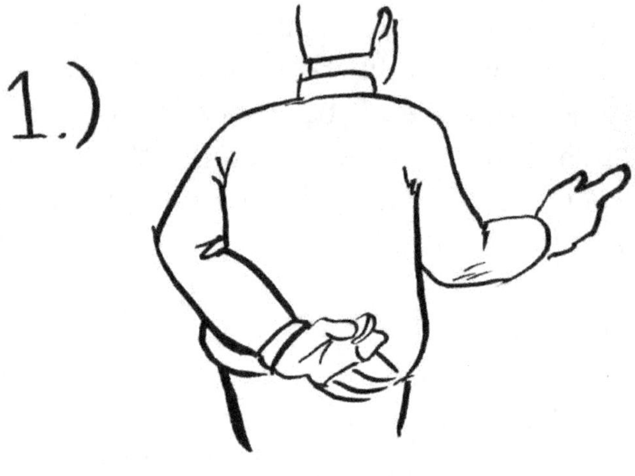

2.)

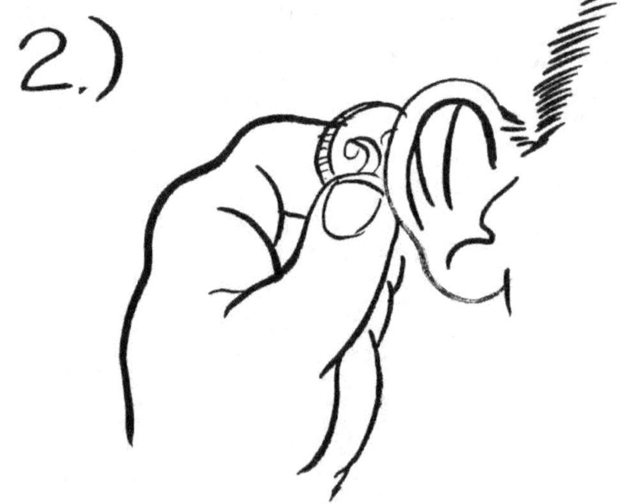

DISAPPEARING SALTSHAKER

To perform this trick you need a saltshaker, large coin and a handkerchief.

First you put a coin on the top of the saltshaker and cover them with a handkerchief. Now grab the saltshaker at the top, lift it up and set it back down a few times. When you do it for the last time drop the saltshaker in your lap and keep only the coin in your hand. Because of it shape it will still look like you are holding a saltshaker under the handkerchief. Act like you are doing magic and crumple up the handkerchief, so everybody will see nothing is under it.

Step by step
1. Put a coin on the top of the saltshaker
2. Cover the saltshaker and the coin with a handkerchief
3. Grab the saltshaker on the top of it and lift it up for a few times
4. Secretly drop the saltshaker in your lap
5. Crumple the handkerchief

MAGIC MAGNETIC FINGERS

To perform this trick you need no special props. Ask someone in the audience to help you. Tell him to put his hands in front of his face and put his pointer fingers tightly together. After a minute tell him that he can slowly pull his fingers apart. His fingers will probably stay together, so you did magnetize his fingers.

Step by step
1. Ask someone in the audience to help you
2. Tell him to out his hands in front of his face
3. Tell him to put his pointer fingers tightly together
4. Wait a minute
5. Tell him to slowly pull his fingers apart

DISAPPEARING COIN

To perform this trick you need a coin, table, small towel and a drinking glass.

First you have to put the glass over the coin, so the coin is inside of the glass, and a towel over the glass. Grab everything together and start doing circles on the table. In one of these circles let the coin slide under the glass into your lap (nobody can see this). Make some more circles and lift up the towel and the glass. The coin has disappeared.

Step by step
1. Place a coin on the table in front of you
2. Put a glass over the coin
3. Put a towel over the glass
4. Grab everything and start making circles with it
5. Secretly lift the glass and let the coin slip into your lap
6. Lift the towel and the glass

1.)

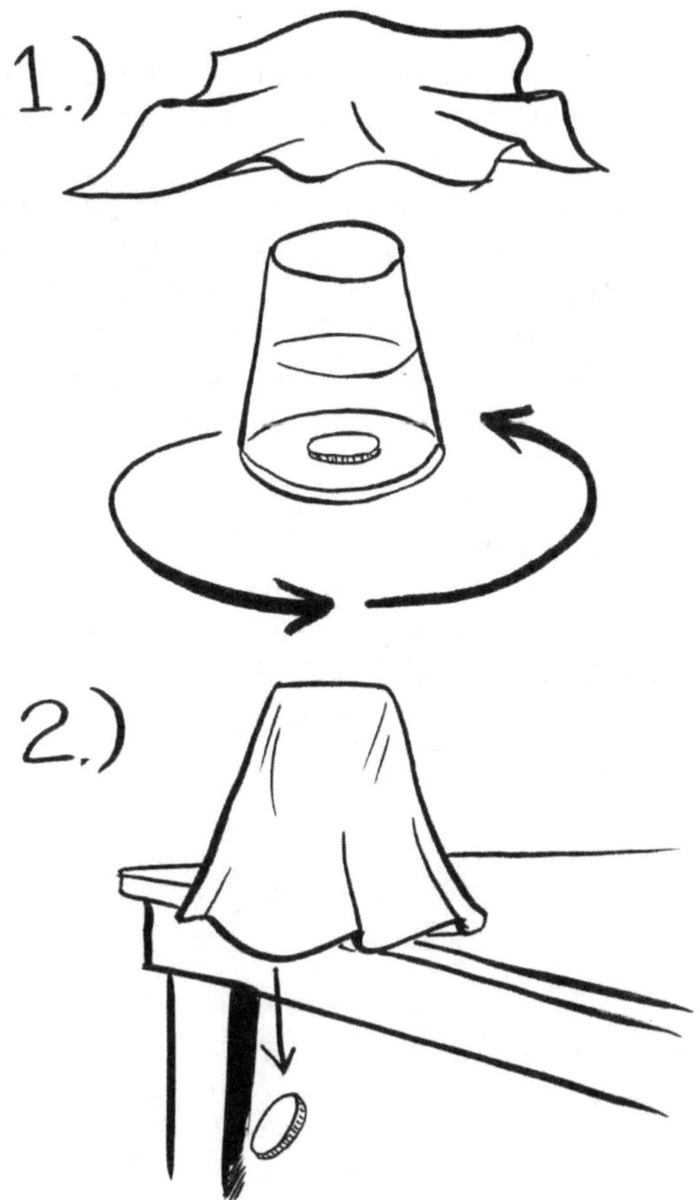

2.)

TURN WATER TO ICE

To perform this trick you need a large plastic cup (colored), ice cube, small sponge and a pitcher of water.

First you have to put the sponge tightly into the cup, so it can't fall out when you move the cup. Now put the ice cube over the sponge. Pour some water into the cup and act like you are doing magic. Turn the cup upside down and amaze everybody because the only thing coming from that cup will be ice cube.

Step by step
1. Put a sponge into the cup
2. Put the ice cube over the sponge
3. Pour water into the cup
4. Turn the cup upside down

1.)

2.)

3.)

APPEARING COIN

To perform this trick you need a coin and a matchbox.

For start you have to open the matchbox halfway and wedge the coin between the drawer and the cover in the back of the matchbox. Hold the matchbox very tightly so the coin won't slip back into the box and show the audience that the box is empty. Now close the matchbox so the coin can slip into it, open it again and show everybody that you made a coin appear in the box.

Step by step

1. Open the matchbox halfway
2. Wedge the coin between the drawer and the cover in the back of the matchbox
3. Show the audience that the matchbox is empty
4. Close the matchbox and let the coin slip into it
5. Show the audience that a coin appears in the matchbox

BREAK YOUR NOSE

To perform this trick you need no special props. To trick the audience you have to cover your nose with both hands, like you are praying. Put your thumbnails behind your front teeth. Now move your hands side to side flicking your fingers from behind the teeth and because of the sound they are making everybody will think that you are breaking your own nose.

Step by step
1. Cover your nose with both hands
2. Put your thumbnails behind your front teeth
3. Move your hands from side to side flicking your fingers from behind your teeth

1.)

2.)

SWITCHING FINGERS

To perform this trick you need a rubber band. For start you have to slide the rubber band over your middle and index fingers, all the way down. Now secretly curl your fingers in a fist and stretch the rubber band over all four fingers. Show to the audience back of your hand so they will think that the rubber band is only around those two fingers. For the end raise your hand and the rubber band should jump to your ring and pinky fingers.

Step by step
1. Slide the rubber band over your middle and index fingers
2. Secretly curl tour fingers to a fist
3. Stretch the rubber band over all four fingers
4. Show to the audience back of your hand
5. Raise your hand and let the rubber band jump on your ring and pinky fingers

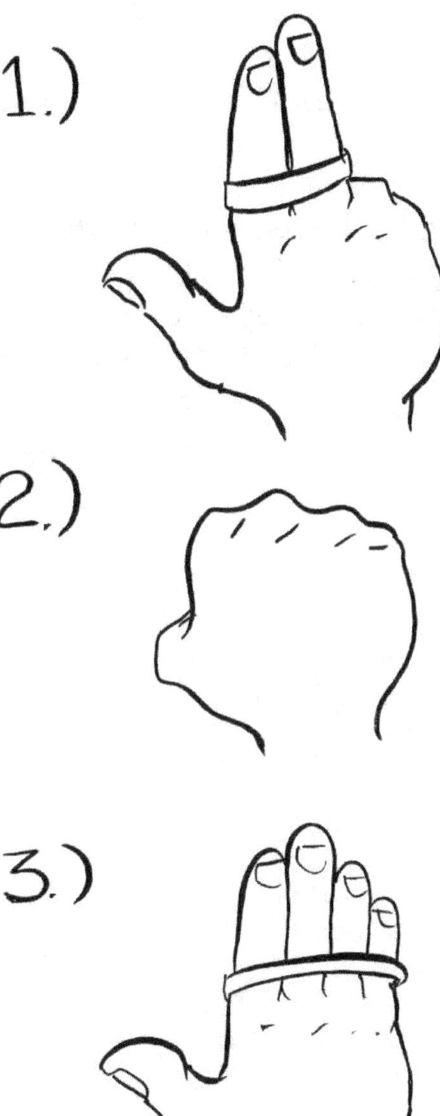

1.)
2.)
3.)

PAPER CLIPS IN LOVE

To perform this trick you need a dollar bill and two paper clips.

Bet the audience that you can link two paper clips together without even touching them. Next fold the dollar bill in thirds and use the paper clips to clip two of the three layers of paper near the open end. Now grab each end of the bill with your hands and quickly pull the ends apart. Two paper clips should fly in the air and linked together when they land.

Step by step
1. Fold the dollar bill in thirds
2. Clip with the paper clips two of the three layers of the bill
3. Grab each end of the bill and pull them apart

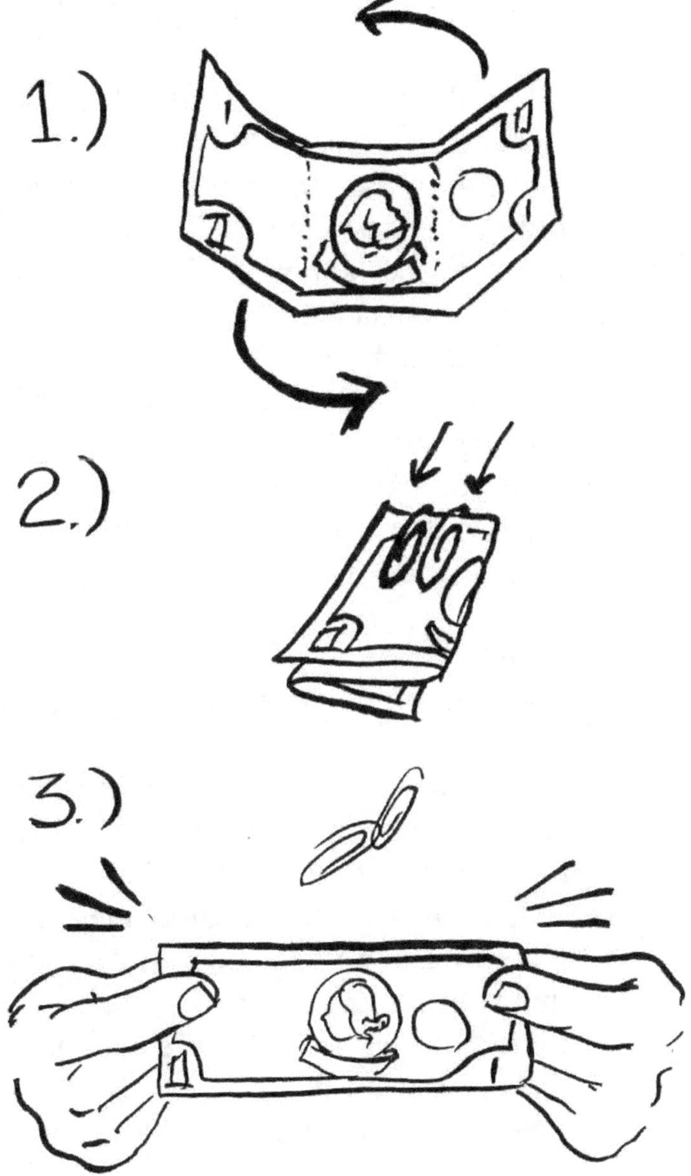

1.)
2.)
3.)

SECRETLY DISAPPEARING COIN

To perform this trick you need a handkerchief, two coins and an assistant.

First you must take each coin in one hand and cover only one hand with the handkerchief. Ask someone from the audience if thye can feel the coin under the handkerchief. Now ask your assistant if he can feel the same coin, only in reality he will secretly take the coin away. Now show to everybody that the coin has disappeared. At the end you can make the coin reappear with replacing the other coin in your other hand into the covered hand and extend the trick.

Step by step
1. Take one coin in one hand and one coin in other hand
2. Cover one hand with the handkerchief
3. Ask someone in the audience if he can feel the coin under the handkerchief
4. Ask your assistant the same question
5. Your assistant has to secretly take away that coin
6. Show to everybody that the coin has disappeared
7. Place the coin in the other hand into the covered hand

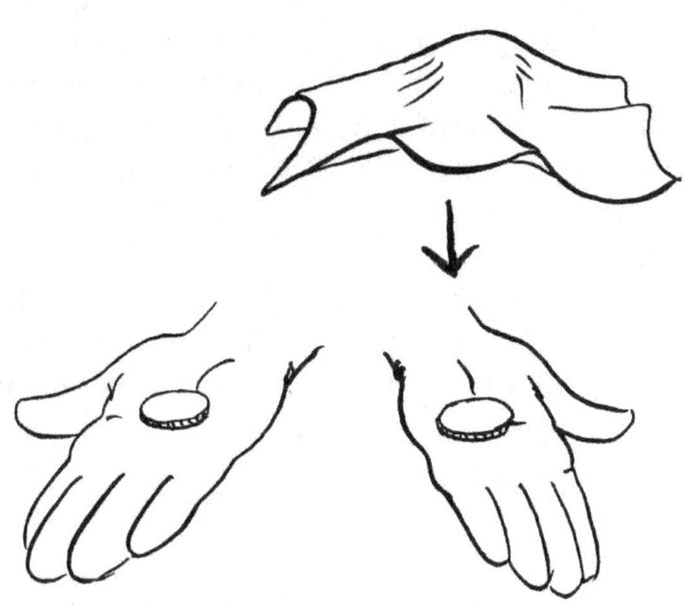

TURNING SALT INTO PEPPER

To perform this trick you need a napkin, saltshaker (full) and a pepper.

At first you have to twist off the cap from the saltshaker and press the napkin into the saltshaker (forming a small well). Now put some pepper in this well and twist the cap back on. Make sure that the napkin doesn't stick out of the saltshaker. Then show the audience the saltshaker and tell them that you can then turn the salt into pepper. Now pour some salt into your palm (in reality you are pouring pepper so don't let anybody see that), close your hand and act like you are doing magic. Now open your hand and show everybody the pepper in it.

Step by step
1. Twist off of the cap on the saltshaker
2. Press the napkin into the saltshaker to form a well
3. Put pepper in the well
4. Twist the cap back on the saltshaker
5. Pour salt into your palm
6. Close your hand
7. Tell everybody some magic words
8. Open your hands

STUCK ROCKS

To perform this trick you need 3 rocks.
Ask someone in the audience to hold two rocks in his hands, pushing them together as hard as possible. Now take the third rock and wave it around the member's hands for eight times. With the same rock touch his knuckles on both hands and tell him to very slowly pull his rocks apart. He won't be able to do it so it will seem like you tied the rocks together.

Step by step
1. Ask someone in the audience to help you
2. Tell him to hold one rock in one hand and one rock in other hand
3. Tell him to push the rocks together
4. Take the third rock
5. Wave with the third rock eight times around your helper's hands
6. Touch with the third rock your helper's knuckles on both hands
7. Tell him to pull his arms apart

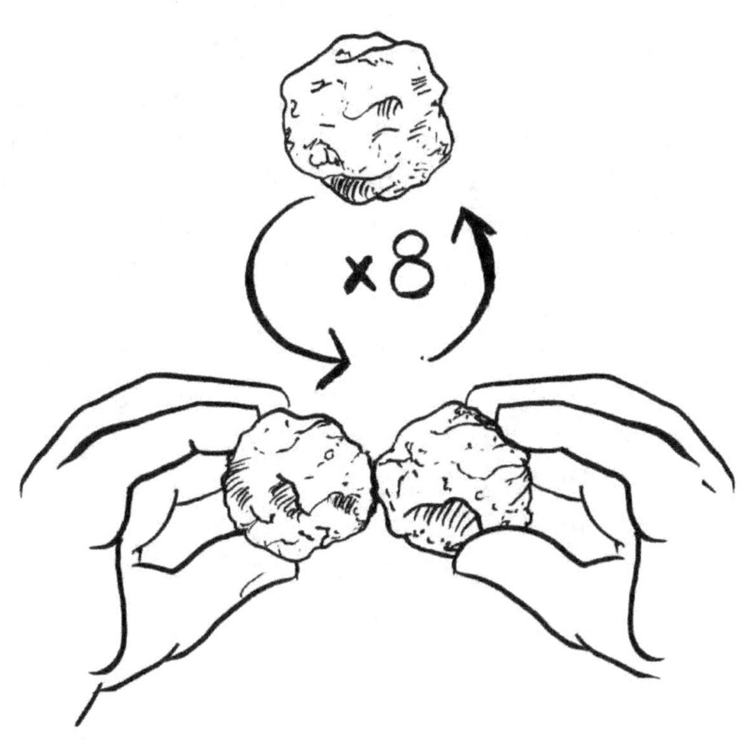

×8

STUCK TO THE CHAIR

To perform this trick you need a chair.

Ask someone from the audience (your secret assistant) to sit in a chair, with both feet on the floor next to each other. Now place your pointer finger in the middle of his forehead and press lightly. Now ask him politely to stand up without using his hands. He won't be able to do it, so you can show everybody your super strong finger.

Step by step
1. Ask someone in the audience to help you
2. Tell him to sit in the chair
3. Place your finger in the middle of his forehead
4. Press lightly with your finger
5. Tell him to stand up

1.)

2.)

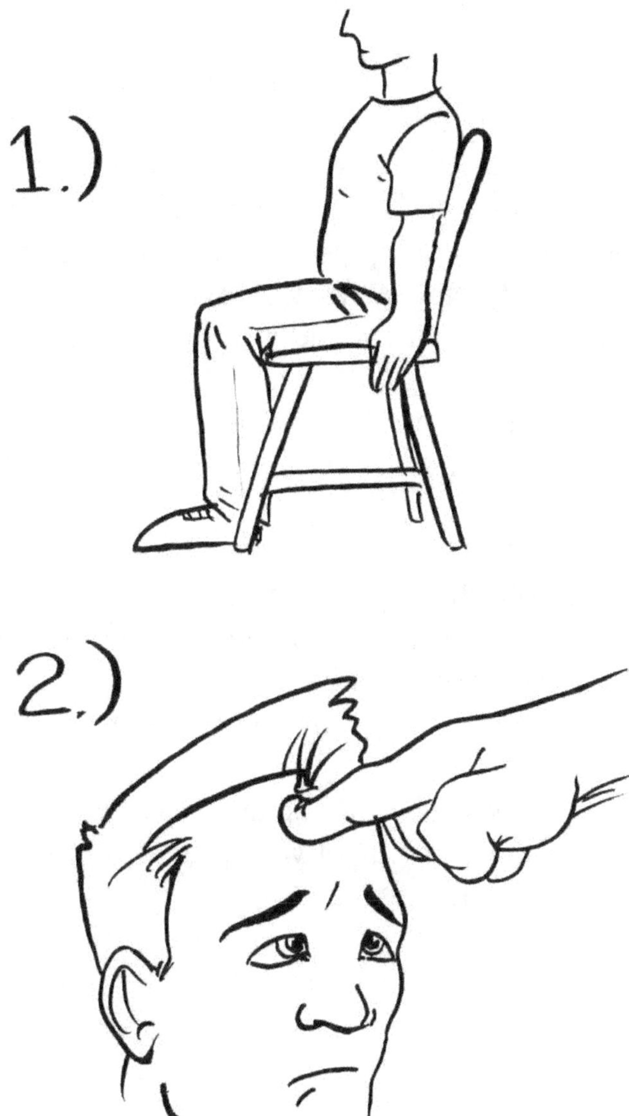

BREAK A CARROT WITH PAPER

To perform this trick you need a carrot (very thin one) and a paper.

First you have to hold the carrot in one hand and a folded paper on half in the other hand. As you are holding the paper put your index finger behind it, but nobody can see that. Now move the paper up and down the carrot and at one point break at half with pressuring it with your index finger. Everybody in the audience will think that you broke the carrot using only the paper.

Step by step
1. Fold the paper on half
2. Hold the carrot in one hand and folded paper in other hand
3. Secretly put your index finger behind the paper
4. Move the paper up and down the carrot
5. Break the carrot with pressuring it with your index finger

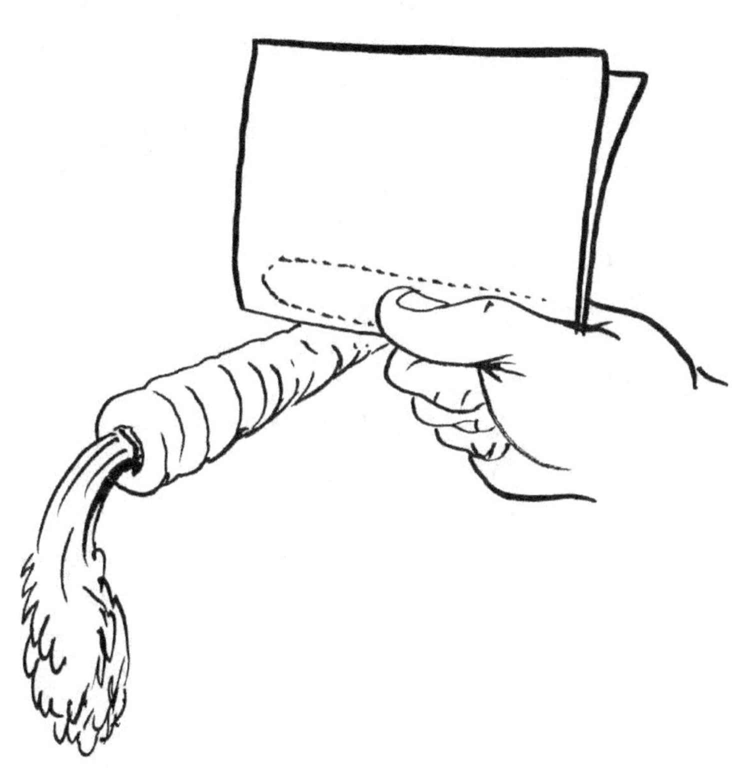

BAGGIE AND PENCIL MAGIC SCIENCE ACTIVITY

To perform this trick you need a zip plastic bag, sharp pencil and a water.

First you have to fill the plastic bag (about 75% of it) with water and seal it tight. Pick up the bag with one hand and push the pen (it should be really very sharp) with its pointy end through the bag with the other hand. You have to push the pen so far that it comes out on the other side of the bag, too. Your audience will be amazed as the pressure means the water will not spill out.

Step by step
1. Fill the plastic bag with a water
2. Seal the plastic bag
3. Pick up the plastic bag
4. With other hand push the pen through the both sides of the bag

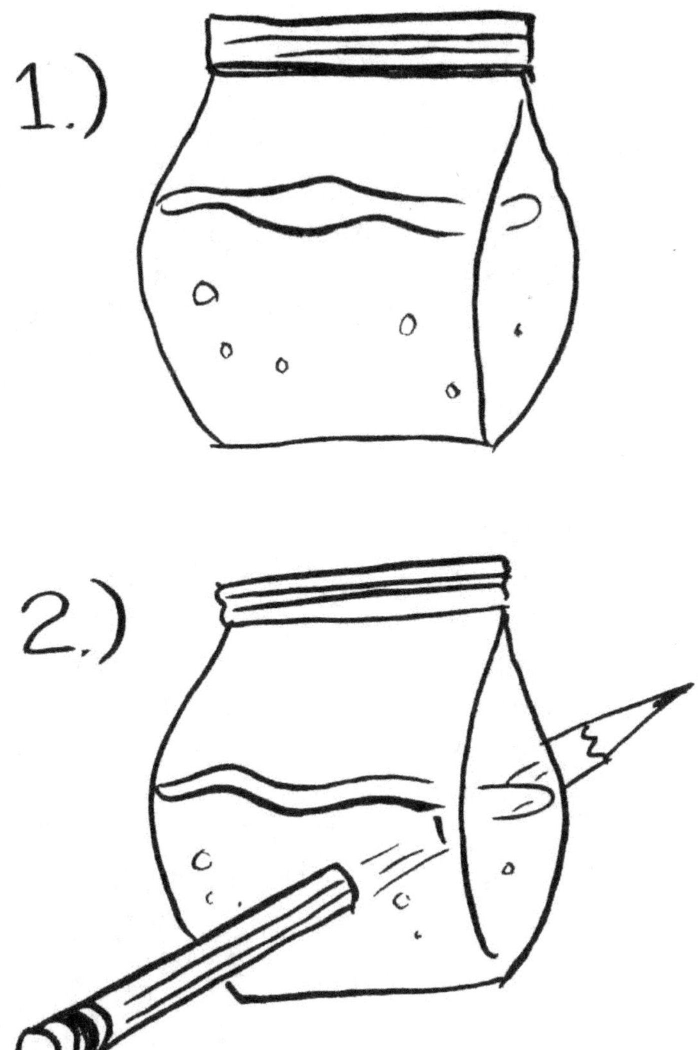

1.)
2.)

WATER STAYS IN UP-SIDE-DOWN GLASS

To perform this trick you need some cardboard, water and a glass.
First you have to fill half of the glass with water. Then tear the cardboard into a square big enough to cover up the rim of the glass. Now place the cardboard square on the top of the glass and turn the glass upside down. Now carefully move your hand from the cardboard and show the audience that the cardboard stayed at its place and is still retaining water in the glass.

Step by step
1. Fill the half of a glass with water
2. Tear the cardboard into a square
3. Place the square on the top of the glass
4. Turn the glass upside down
5. Move your hand away from the cardboard

1.)

2.)

HANDS UP

To perform this trick you need only a wall.
Ask someone in the audience to assist you with this trick. Tell him to place his hands against the wall, palm down, and to lean whit all his weight on his arm. After one minute ask him to step away from the wall. Now you tell him these words: arms rise. His arm will automatically rise in the air.

Step by step
1. Ask someone in the audience to help you
2. Tell him to place his hands against the wall
3. Tell him to lean on his arms with all his weight
4. Wait for one minute
5. Ask him to step away from the wall
6. Say to him: arm rise

1.)

2.)

AMAZING DISAPPEARING PEN TRICK

To perform this trick you need a pen and a table. For start put a pen on the table in front of you. Show the audience that this is an ordinary pen, not magical. Now put both hands on the pen, each hand on each end, palm down. Move the hand with the pen in it towards yourself and drop it in your lap (nobody can see that). Act like the pen is still in your hands and try to break it. When you succeed show the audience that your hands are empty and you made the pen disappear.

Step by step
1. Put a pen on the table in front of you
2. Put both hands on the pen
3. Move the hands with pen in it towards yourself and secretly drop the pen in your lap
4. Act like you are trying to break a pen
5. Show your hands

1.)

2.)

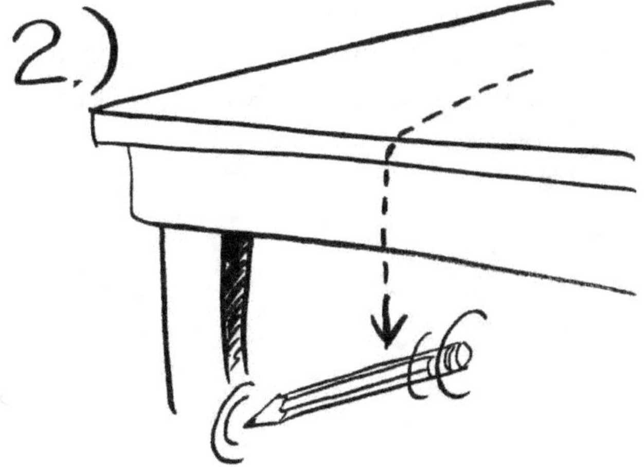

BENDING A COIN

To perform this trick you need a coin.

For start you have hold the coin with both hands on both sides of it, with thumbs on the back side and with index and middle fingers on front side. Now move your hands inwards so that the backs of your hands move forward and towards each other. Your thumbs should be on the coin all the time. Then you move hands into the first position. Repeat this move for a few times in rhythm. An optical illusion witll make the coin appear to bend.

Step by step
1. Hold the coin with both hands on both sides of it
2. Move your hands inwards
3. Move your hands in the first position
4. Repeat same move for a few times in rhythm

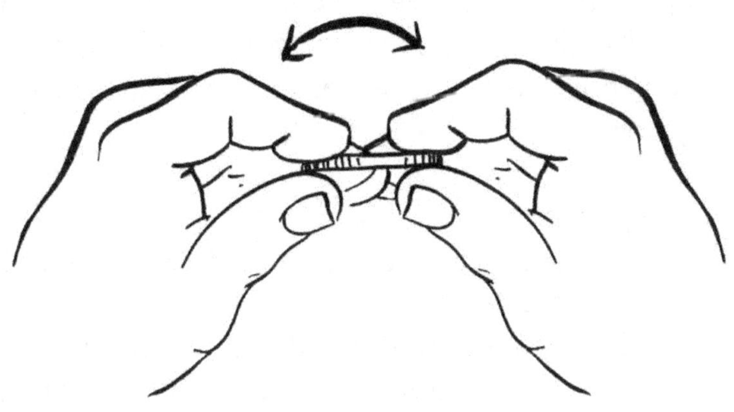

CLICKING SHOULDER MAGIC TRICK

To perform this trick you need a disposable plastic cup.

First you have to place the plastic cup under your arm and squeeze it lightly, so it stays in place but doesn't make any noise. Now put your other hand behind your neck and make an awkward move. As you do that squeeze the cup under your other hand and make some noise with it. It will appear like the noise is coming because you stretched your neck.

Step by step
1. Place a plastic cup under your arm and squeeze it
2. Put your other hand behind your neck
3. Make an awkward move with your hand that is behind your neck
4. Squeeze the cup under your other hand

DISAPPEARING COIN MAGIC TRICK

To perform this trick you need a coin and a table. First you have to place a coin on the table in front of you. Cover the coin with your hand (palm down) and sweep the coin towards you. Quickly sweep it off the table so it looks like you have it in your hand but in reality let it drop in your lap. Now bring your hand up to your mouth and blow up in it. Now open your hand and show that you made a coin disappear.

Step by step
1. Place a coin on the table in front of you
2. Cover the coin with your hand (palm down)
3. Sweep the coin towards you
4. Sweep the coin off the table, but in reality drop it secretly ion your lap
5. Bring your hand to your mouth and blow up in it
6. Open your hand

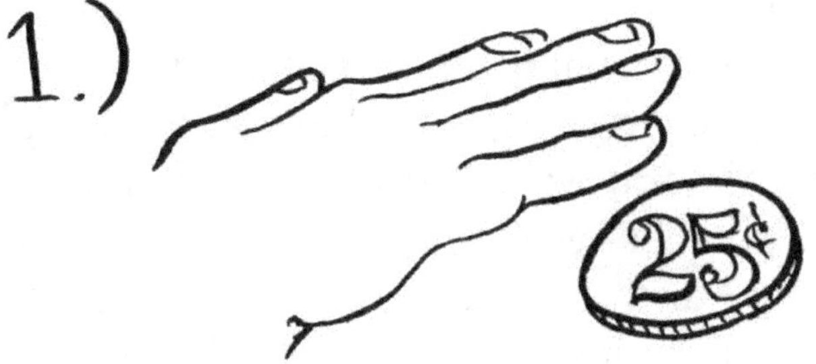
1.)
25¢

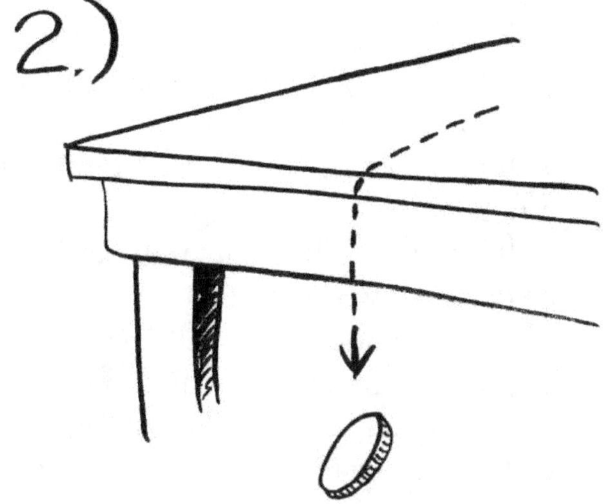
2.)

GUESS THE NUMBER

To perform this trick you need a calculator and paper.

Ask someone in the audience to enter any number (up to seven digit) into the calculator and at the same time to write it down. Tell him to multiply that number by 3, add 2 and multiply that by 3 again. For the end add the number that is greater for 2 than the first number and write down the result. You check the result and if you leave out the last digit of the result you get the number that the member of the audience made up at the beginning.

Step by step
1. Ask someone in the audience to help you
2. Tell him to enter any number (up to seven digits) into the calculator
3. Tell him to write that same number down on the paper
4. Tell him to multiply his number in the calculator by 3 (result 1)
5. Tell him to add 2 to result 1 (result 2)
6. Tell him to multiply result 2 by 3 (result 3)
7. Tell him that he add to result 3 the number that is greater for 2 than his original, first number (final result)
8. Check the result

9. Leave out the last digit and the remaining
    number is your helper's original number

1.)

2.)

GUESS WHICH COIN

To perform this trick you need a several coins. Prepare five or six coins with different dates on them and lay them out on the table. Ask somebody in the audience to help you. Turn away from the table and tell him to choose one coin and memorize the date on it. Tell him to put the coin back with the others coins. Then you turn around and start to examine the coins. The coin that the member of the audience picked up should be the warmest of them all, so this is how you know which coin was picked up. When you find the coin remember the date on it and tell to the audience which coin was selected.

Step by step
1. Ask someone in the audience to help you
2. Place six coins with different dates on them on the table
3. Tell the helper to choose one coin and memorize the date on it
4. Tell him to put his coin back on the table with others coins
5. Turn around and start examine the coins
6. Find his coin and tell the date on it to the audience

MAGIC WAND

To perform this trick you need a pen, ruler, sheet of newspaper, black marker and a paper.

First you have to make a line at each end of the paper (2 cm from the end). Then you color the center of the paper, roll it up and glue it together so it looks like a magic wand. Tell your audience that you can make the wand disappear. Lay it in the center of the sheet of the newspaper, roll it up so nobody can see it and scrunch up the newspaper into a tiny ball. Everyone will be amazed how you did that.

Step by step
1. Make a line at each end of the paper, 2 cm from the end
2. Color the center of the paper
3. Roll up the paper
4. Glue the paper together
5. Lay the rolled paper in the center if the newspaper
6. Roll up the newspaper
7. Scrunch the newspaper into a small ball

1.)

2.)

3.)

THE AMAZING BALANCING COIN

To perform this trick you need a coin and a toothpick.

First you have to snap a toothpick in half and put it in an upright position between your ring and middle fingers. Then push it back so the toothpick lies hidden between your fingers. Now put the coin over your fingers so it lays on the toothpick. Raise the coin to a standing position near the ends of your fingers and at the same time raise the toothpick, too, so it supports the coin behind it, impossible to see for everybody else. Keep the pressure on the toothpick to keep the coin in balance.

Step by step
1. Snap a toothpick in half
2. Put the toothpick in upright position between your ring and middle fingers
3. Push the toothpick back so it lies hidden between the fingers
4. Put the coin over your fingers, so it lays on the toothpick
5. Raise the coin to a standing position and at the same time raise the toothpick, too, to support the coin
6. Keep the pressure on the toothpick

1.)

2.)

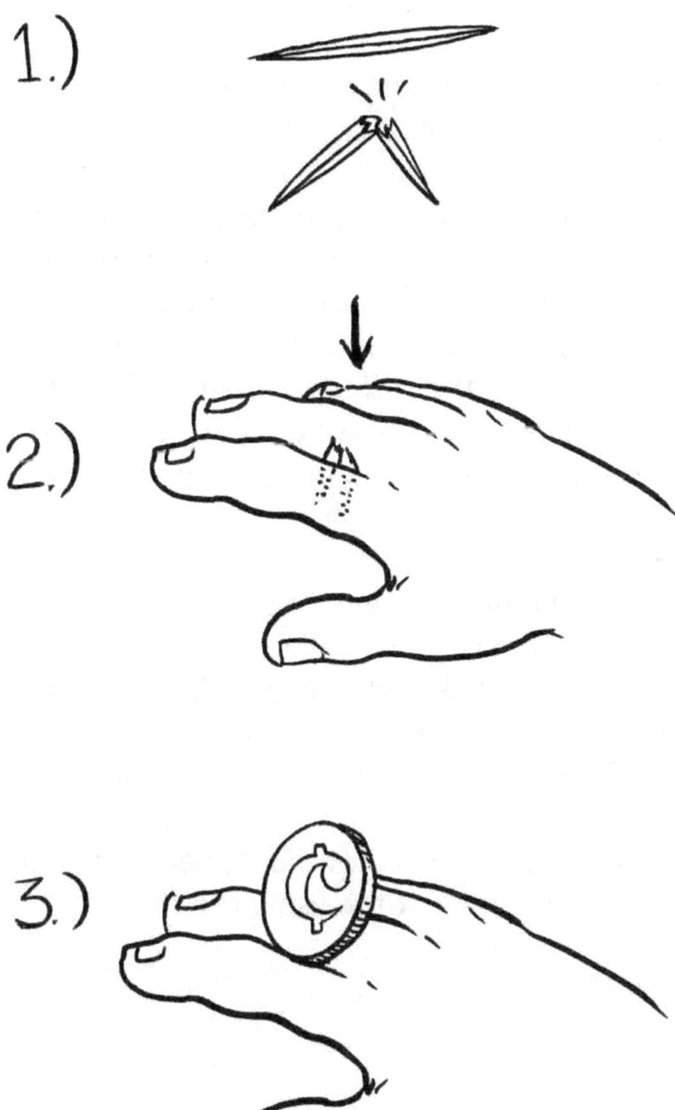

3.)

MAGIC TOUCH

To perform this trick you need an aluminum pie plate, water, toothpicks and a dish detergent.
First you have to fill the plate with a little water, so only the bottom is covered. Now put in the water (in the center of a plate) a few toothpicks (in the shape of a square) and make sure that they overlap (so they stay together). Secretly dip one toothpick in the dish detergent and place it with one end in the middle of the square and watch how the soap will make them drive apart of each other.

Step by step
1. Fill the aluminum pie plate with a little water (cover the bottom of it)
2. Put a few toothpicks in the center of the plate in the shape of a square
3. Secretly dip one toothpick in the dish detergent
4. Place one end of the dipped toothpick in the middle of the square

1.)
2.)
3.)
H₂O

QUICK SWITCH

To perform this trick you need a tape and a paper. First you have to tear the paper in two little pieces (no bigger than your fingernails) and tape each piece to one fingernail on each hand. Then tell the audience that you will make the paper disappear and reappear. Now place your two fingers with the paper in front of you on the table and one at the time put your hands behind your back, quickly switching fingers and putting a finger without paper on it back to the table. Same thing repeat with the other hand. Do the same thing but now you replace the fingers without the paper on it with the fingers with the paper on, so you make the paper reappear.

Step by step
1. Tear the sheet of paper in two pieces (no bigger than your fingernails)
2. Tape each piece to one fingernail on each hand
3. Place two fingers with the paper on them on the table in front of you
4. Put your hands behind your back (one at the time)
5. Quickly switch the fingers from the one with the paper on it to the one with no paper on it

6. Put the hands back on the table

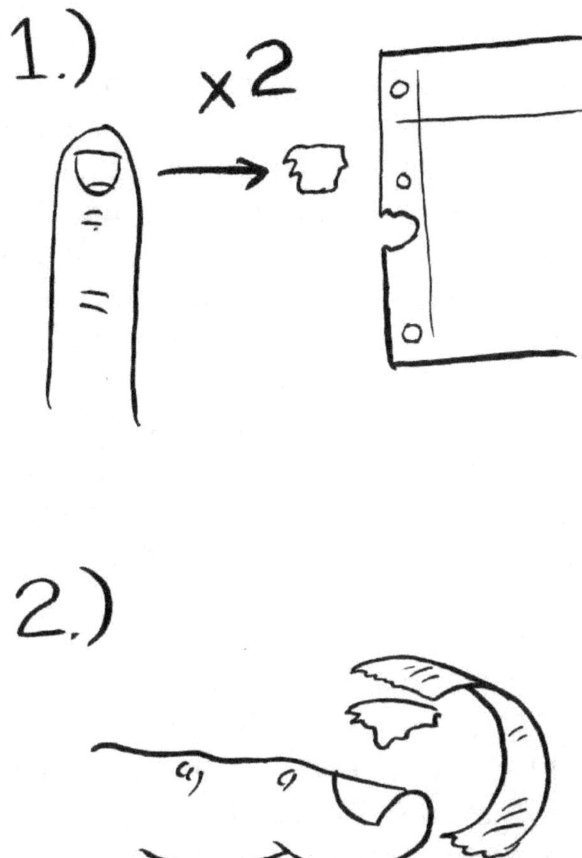

ALL FALL DOWN

To perform this trick you need dishtowel, plastic cup and an eraser.

At first you put the eraser on the table in front of you, cover it up with the cup and then place a dishtowel on top of everything. Now lift the dishtowel and cup together so the eraser is revealed on the table. Ask the audience to concentrate on the eraser and while they are doing that you secretly drop the cup in your lap. Then put the dishtowel back over the eraser and really hard smash your hand down on it. At exactly the same time drop the cup on the floor and show everybody that the dishtowel and eraser are still on the table but the cup felt through it on the floor.

Step by step
1. Put the eraser on the table in front of you
2. Cover the eraser with a cup
3. Place a dishtowel over the cup and eraser
4. Lift the dishtowel and the cup
5. Secretly drop the cup on your lap
6. Put the dishtowel back over the eraser
7. Smash the dishtowel with your hand and at the same time drop the cup under on the floor